Reading Readiness

The advisory editor to the series is John E. Merritt, Professor of Educational Studies, The Open University, Milton Keynes.

Reading Readiness

John Downing and Derek Thackray

HODDER AND STOUGHTON
London   Sydney   Auckland   Toronto
for the United Kingdom Reading Association

Acknowledgments

We wish to thank Colleen Hills and Linda Cleough for their careful preparation of the manuscript, and Marianne and Rupert Downing for their help in reading the manuscript. We also wish to thank Mrs Lucy Thackray for the drawings on pages 100 to 102.

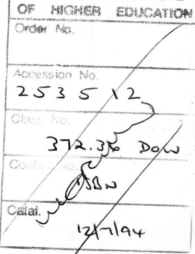

ISBN 0 340 19978 4

First published 1971
Second edition copyright © 1975 John Downing
and Derek Thackray
Second impression 1976

Printed and bound in Great Britain for
Hodder and Stoughton Educational,
a division of Hodder and Stoughton Ltd, London,
by Hazell Watson & Viney Ltd, Aylesbury, Bucks

Contents

Preface

So many books are being published in the education field today that it is very difficult for teachers to keep in touch with research and new developments. This series of monographs has been devised both to collate new ideas and to save teachers of reading from having to spend much of their valuable time searching out relevant texts and materials.

Each monograph will deal with a specific problem area (for example, modern innovations in teaching reading, reading readiness, the development of fluency, problems of assessment), giving a review of theoretical considerations and published research, and pointing out their important practical implications.

Professor J. E. Merritt
Department of Educational Studies
The Open University, Milton Keynes

Chapter 1 Definitions and Evolution of the Concept of 'Reading Readiness'

The term 'readiness' for any kind of learning refers to the stage firstly, when the child can learn easily and without emotional strain, and secondly, when the child can learn profitably because efforts at teaching give gratifying results. Note that 'readiness' does not necessarily imply that a child achieves this state only through growth or maturation. He may also arrive at readiness through having completed the prior learning on which the new learning will be based.

It is important to note also that since readiness is a general concept which can be applied to a pupil's preparedness to undertake any particular learning task, it must be applicable to various stages of learning to read from the beginning right up to the most sophisticated forms of reading which may not be fully learned until the individual reaches adulthood. Learning to read is a continuous developmental process and readiness is a valid concept for many stages in it. However, this book will focus attention on readiness for the earliest beginning stage of what is sometimes termed 'formal reading'.

Definitions of the term 'reading' are many and often contrasting as the following examples from Latham (1968),* show:

'Reading involves nothing more than the correlation of a sound image with its corresponding visual image . . .' (Bloomfield and Barnhart, 1961).

'Reading is the art of reconstructing from the printed page, the writer's ideas, feelings, moods and sensory impressions.' (Artley 1961).

These two examples show how definitions of reading vary in two typical ways. Some (like Artley's) are very comprehensive while others (like that of Bloomfield and Barnhart) are very narrow. Some specify the connection between the sounds of language and their visual form in print or writing (as does the definition of Bloomfield and Barnhart), but other authors seem to prefer not to specify this aspect.

An excellent discussion of this question as to what exactly we mean by the term 'reading' has been provided by Dearden (1967). He shows that, for normal hearing and speaking people,

* All references are given on pp. 103 ff.

9

reading certainly must involve some connection between the spoken and written forms of language. Obviously, in oral reading it does. On the other hand, you could open a book at its last page and read it aloud backwards until you came to the top of the first page. In this way you would have 'read' every word in the book, but you could hardly say that you had 'read the book', as Dearden points out.

The view of the authors of this book is that 'reading' is all that variety of behaviour which ordinary people include when they say that someone 'is reading'. This includes the translation of print into both the sounds of spoken language as well as their meaning. Both are very important from the beginning. Therefore, our definition of reading at the early stages of learning is that it is the recognition of the auditory and semantic significance of printed or written words. To learn to read, the young beginner must decode the print by translating it into the spoken form of the language and into its linguistic meaning.

We may now combine our definitions of 'readiness' and 'reading'. *Reading readiness is defined as the stage in development when, either through maturation or through previous learning, or both, the individual child can learn to read easily and profitably.*

Although the specific term 'readiness' is relatively new in education, being first used in the 'Report of the National Committee on Reading', *Twenty-fourth Year Book of the National Society for the Study of Education* (1925), the concept undoubtedly goes back at least two hundred years.

In the seventeenth century, educational thinkers such as Comenius and Locke had already recognised that the child himself should be the determining factor in the educational process, but their views were not typical of the age. Rousseau in 1762, made a more arresting statement of this truth, and in his book *Émile* (translated by B. Foxley 1957) can be seen the crude, but nevertheless clear, beginnings of the readiness concept. Rousseau felt that education should be accommodated to the various stages of the child's development. He rejected the formal teaching of the schools and educated Émile according to nature:

'Give nature time to work before you take over her business lest you interfere with her dealings. You assert that you know the value of time and are afraid to waste it. You fail to perceive that it is a greater waste of time to use it ill than to do nothing, and that a child ill taught is further from virtue than a child who has learnt nothing at all.'

To educate according to nature was one of Rousseau's fundamental principles, and, throughout *Émile*, he expresses this principle both positively and negatively. Examples of positive statements are:

'There is a time for every kind of teaching and we ought to recognize it, and each has its own dangers to be avoided.'

'Every stage, every station in life has a perfection of its own.'

Examples of negative statements are:

'Nothing is useful and good for him which is unbefitting to his age.'

'Beware of anticipating teaching which demands more maturity of mind.'

In these quotations can be seen the beginnings of the readiness concept, beginnings which later writers clarified and brought to the experimental stage.

Pestalozzi (1898) was much influenced by Rousseau's writings and actually tried to put some of his ideas into practice at his private schools at Stanz (1798–99), Burgdorf (1799–1804) and Yverdon (1805–1827). He felt that the educator's duty was to assist nature's development so as to secure a natural and harmonious progress. This idea is expressed in the following quotation from his book, *How Gertrude Teaches Her Children*:

'All instruction of man is then only the art of helping nature to develop in her own way: and this art rests essentially on the relation and harmony between the impression received by the child and the exact degree of his developed powers. It is also necessary in the impressions that are brought to the child by instruction that there should be a sequence so that the beginning and progress should keep pace with the beginning and progress of the powers to be developed in the child.'

Froebel (1887) strengthened and added to the ideas of Rousseau and Pestalozzi. As a scientist he was impressed by Darwin's theory of evolution, and saw the human being as a biological organism for which education needed only to provide nourishment and freedom. The following quotation from his book, *The Education of Man*, illustrates this point:

'All the child is ever to be and become, lies, however slightly educated, in the child, and can be attained only through development from within outward.'

Froebel stressed that the child's growth was one of steady continuous development; this idea is only one step away from stressing that each child has its own individual pattern of growth and rate of maturation, an idea vital to the concept of readiness.

However, until Dewey made his ideas felt, the readiness concept was only indicated in the writings of a small minority of educators and philosophers. Dewey crystallised the concept and stated it in vigorous terms again and again so that educators in many countries felt the impact of his convictions. In an article on primary education, Dewey (1898) discussed at length the subject of a child's readiness for language study in the primary grades, without actually mentioning the specific term. In it he states:

'Present physiological knowledge points to the age of about eight years as early enough for anything more than an incidental attention to visual and written language form.'

Patrick (1899), a disciple of Dewey, helped to popularise his master's ideas, and, in an article on readiness, he states:

'Our increasing knowledge of the child's mind, his muscular and nervous system, and his special senses points indubitably to the conclusion that reading and writing are subjects which do not belong to the early years of school life, but to a later period.'

During the first twenty-five years of this present century, three important influences helped to give a firm foundation to the readiness concept among our accepted educational principles. Firstly, Dewey's (1909, 1916, 1926) influence began to make itself felt during these years, in which he published his most important books. Secondly, experimental psychologists such as Thorndike (1913) and Terman (1919) in America, Burt (1922) and Ballard (1922) in Britain were evolving procedures for conducting experiments and devising tools of measurement and statistical techniques for research related to this problem. Finally, concern was being expressed in America at the low standards of reading, and the first specialists in the field of reading instruction began to make their appearance. Huey's (1908) *The Psychology and Pedagogy of Reading* was the first professional book on the teaching of reading, but it was quickly followed by others.

In 1925, the *Twenty-fourth Year Book of the National Society for the Study of Education* was published in the U.S.A. Before this date the concept of readiness evolved slowly over a long period, but from 1925 onwards began a period of intensive application and investigation of reading readiness in America. It is generally agreed that the specific term 'readiness' was used for the first time in this Year Book, which recognised the problem of reading readiness and suggested methods of diagnosing and remedying deficiencies in readiness. This book was widely distributed and it exerted a very strong influence in initiating the preparatory period preceding first grade reading.

The most influential study of reading readiness was that of Morphett and Washburne (1931), and, from about that date, experimental studies of various aspects of readiness became extremely numerous, growing rapidly year by year, until the years 1938–40 were reached, possibly the peak period for investigation into the nature of the concept.

In America, the number of investigations and articles concerned with reading readiness declined in the 1940s and 1950s. The main reason for this was not because it was felt that all the important aspects had been dealt with adequately, but because of a shift of emphasis with regard to readiness. Factors contributing to readiness for beginning to read were found to be the same factors which contribute to reading success at later levels, and so the readiness concept was applied to all stages of growth in reading and at all levels of maturation.

But in the 1960s came a revival of interest in the concept of reading readiness on both sides of the Atlantic. In Britain during that period, there was a general increase in interest in the teaching of reading which was associated with the re-examination of the concept of reading readiness. In the United States during the same period there was also a marked interest in re-opening the issue of reading readiness, but for a different reason. It seems to have been related more in America to a growing dissatisfaction with the results of the stereotyped mass education procedures of the grade system in the schools of American public education. The discontent, however, was not directed at the mass production methods of schooling. Instead it tended to focus on what was felt to be the slow progress made by the majority of pupils. A general concern for the lack of individualization in the teaching methods used in American schools was not noticeable during the 1960s, although towards the end of the decade more and more writers drew attention to this common weakness in the usual American system of grade levels.

Diack (1960) expresses well the impatience which many American educators were beginning to feel with the mass application of rules of reading readiness:

'In America particularly, the actual teaching of reading has been so much delayed that many a child, instead of getting ready to read, gets bored with waiting to be taught.'

It is interesting to reflect on the educational approach and teaching methods implied by Diack's final phrase 'waiting to be taught'. It certainly indicates a very different view of education to that of Rousseau who laid the foundations of this concept.

It also suggests an important difference in the outlook of British and American teachers as regards readiness. A British primary school where children 'waited to be taught' something they were ready to learn for themselves would have been a comparatively rare entity even in the early 1960s.

However, the view of readiness which is more typical of the modern British primary school, has received its most outspoken support from an American psychologist, Bruner (1960):

'The foundations of any subject may be taught to anybody at any age in some form.'

He shows that by 'in some form', he is proposing that the concept of readiness implies adaptation by the teacher to the child's level of development.

Thus the concept of readiness has evolved, and, although it has branched out in various directions, yet, in Bruner's work, it has found a new dynamic expression of Rousseau's original thesis.

FACTORS IN READING READINESS

Our definition of reading readiness referred to the 'stage in development when, either through maturation or through previous learning, or both the individual child can learn. . . .' There are many abilities, skills, influences and interests which may develop through maturation or learning and thereby contribute in some measure to the stage of readiness for beginning to learn to read. Some authorities produce long lists of specific traits and influences that determine a child's readiness for reading; most writers group these traits and influences under a small number of broad headings. Harrison (1939), and Inglis (1949), use the three broad headings of physiological, intellectual and personal readiness; Smith (1950), Hildreth (1958) and Schonell (1961), use physiological readiness and intellectual readiness but sub-divide personal readiness further, using such headings as social, emotional, experiential, linguistic and environmental readiness. Yoakam (1955), quotes Durrell as having said:

'Each of us likes his own analysis of the factors in reading.
Dr Yoakam may list sixty-four and I will list eighteen. He likes his and I like mine.'

The grouping of influences on reading readiness is obviously an arbitrary one, but there are certain factors which are generally recognised and discussed in this literature. These generally recognised factors will be dealt with in this book under the following four headings:

14

1 *Physiological factors*, including general maturity and growth; cerebral dominance and laterality; neurological considerations; vision; hearing; condition and functioning of speech organs (Chapter 2).

2 *Environmental factors*, including linguistic background of the home and social experiences of different kinds (Chapter 3).

3 *Emotional, motivational and personality factors*, including emotional stability and a desire to learn to read (Chapter 4).

4 *Intellectual factors*, including general mental ability, the perceptual abilities of visual and auditory discrimination, and the special reasoning and thinking abilities involved in solving problems in learning to read (Chapter 5).

In order to find out the relative importance and the predictive value of various reading readiness measures, American research workers have usually given tests and made assessments when the children concerned were at the beginning of the First Grade (about six years of age). A few months later and perhaps again a year later, reading achievement tests usually have been given to the same children and the later results correlated with the earlier results. The coefficients of correlation obtained by this procedure are generally accepted as measures of the importance of the particular readiness factor for later success in learning to read. The higher the correlation between the readiness factor and subsequent reading achievement, the more important is said to be the contribution of that readiness factor. In the chapters which follow we will have recourse to this type of correlational research many times. But we need to be aware of its limitations and the logical error to which such correlational studies all too often lead. When two aspects of human experience or behaviour are statistically related there is no guarantee that one aspect causes the other. We must not jump too easily to such a conclusion.

We shall also examine other types of research evidence, and we will refer to expert opinions if no more objective data are available. In this way, we shall examine all the possibly important factors in reading readiness which have been studied by various educational theorists and research workers. Sometimes the evidence will be negative, thus indicating that the proposed reading readiness factor is of no practical importance to the teacher. We hope that readers of this book will patiently explore with us all these possibilities. It is valuable to know what factors are *not* very important as well as those that are.

Chapter 2 Physiological Factors

GENERAL MATURITY

Research focussed on the relationship between reading and reading readiness, and the total growth or level of maturity of the child was stimulated by the work of Olson (1940), and his associates at the University of Michigan who developed the idea that reading achievement is a function of general maturity, or total growth, and conversely that reading failure stems from immaturity. Their studies have featured the longitudinal method of research, in which periodic measurements of the same group of children are taken over a long stretch of time. The measurements made are usually those of height, weight, strength of grip, teeth erupted, hand and wrist bones as well as educational achievement. Longitudinal studies of this kind reveal that individual differences in these measurements tend to persist over a period of time, and that growth manifests some unity when viewed as a whole. An individual's educational achievement was found to fall within his area of total growth pattern and this finding led to the hypothesis that 'achievement is the function of the organism as a whole'. Olson and Hughes (1942), have used the term 'organismic age' to represent the average of a certain number of growth ages at one particular time. The ages they use to average for this concept are mental age, dental age, reading age, weight age, height age, carpal age (hand and wrist bones) and grip age. Olson and Hughes argue that the child's reading achievement is linked to his 'organismic age', though they point out that there is no easy formula for the number or selection of measurements needed for an adequate organismic age. In one longitudinal study of 28 boys and 28 girls, Olson draws this conclusion:

'When for the purposes of contrast one views the highest boy and the highest girl, and the lowest boy and the lowest girl, in the series, one secures a most dramatic picture of the generalisation that reading tends to be an aspect of the growth of the child as a whole.'

In support of this view, Anderson and Hughes (1955), have shown from a study of matched groups of boys and girls in the first grade, that success in reading at this early stage is a function of total development; the results suggested that children who are advanced in general maturity succeed in reading, and those who are retarded physically tend to fail in reading. However, other studies over a fairly long period, for example, those of Gates (1924), Abernethy (1936), Dearborn and Rothney (1941), and Blommers, Knief and Stroud (1955), have investigated the relationship between mental and physical growth, and have found only a very slight relationship with low correlations between mental and physical measurements. Stroud (1956), points out that rarely do these correlation coefficients exceed ·20, of which figure he says: 'The predictive value of coefficients of this magnitude is negligible, being less than 2 per cent better than chance.' He comes to the conclusion that anatomical and physiological growth are related neither to reading achievement nor to mental development.

Thus the results of research into the relationship between reading and general maturity appear to provide conflicting evidence. We must conclude, therefore, that there is little evidence to support the view that general maturity is an important factor in readiness to read.

SEX DIFFERENCES IN READING READINESS AND EARLY READING

Girls and boys are obviously different physiologically and so it has often been proposed that their different biological constitutions cause differences in their attainments in reading and writing. Usually, it has been theorised that girls tend to mature earlier than boys physically, intellectually and emotionally, and so may be ready to read earlier than boys and to stay ahead in reading during the ensuing years. Anderson and Dearborn (1951), and Harris (1961), point out that girls tend to reach puberty about one and a half years earlier than boys, and from birth on there are detectable differences in physiological maturity, particularly as shown by the date of appearance of teeth and by the ossification of the skeleton. Similarly, with regard to language development, McCarthy (1935) shows that by the twentieth month of life girls are superior in the production of speech sounds, and also that girls begin to talk somewhat earlier than boys and their childhood vocabularies are larger.

Some studies have examined the difference in readiness to read between boys and girls entering school, and also the difference between their respective achievements during the first year in school. Most American investigations, among the more important being those of Samuels (1943), Carroll (1948), Prescott (1955), and Anderson, Hughes and Dixon (1957), show significant differences between boys and girls on reading readiness measures in favour of the girls, though one or two other investigators, for example Potter (1949), and Konski (1955), found no significant differences.

In Thackray's (1965) first experiment with 182 British children the scores of the girls were significantly superior to those of the boys on two of the five reading readiness measures, namely, those of auditory discrimination and using the context and auditory clues. However in Thackray's (1971) experiment a comparison between the mean scores attained by the boys and girls on the reading readiness measures given initially showed no significant differences. Thus the evidence from America and Britain gives contradictory conclusions concerning the differences between boys and girls with regard to reading readiness.

Once children are able to read, then American research also shows quite clearly that in that country girls have a superiority over boys in the normal classroom situation, e.g., Durrell (1940) and Gates (1961). This finding has been confirmed by the evidence from the large scale research reported by Dykstra and Tinney (1969). They compared 1 659 boys and 1 624 girls from schools in Pennsylvania, Michigan, New York, and New Jersey. A great deal of data was collected on reading readiness as well as on reading achievements in first and second grades. The statistical evidence unquestionably shows the superiority of American girls both in readiness and in later reading. The authors' conclusion is:

'This study yielded further support to the mass of evidence which demonstrates that girls have more advanced visual and auditory discrimination abilities at the readiness stage and are superior in reading ability, spelling ability, conventions of language (usage and punctuation) and arithmetic computation through the second grade.'

The evidence from research workers in Britain concerning the relative performance of boys and girls on reading tests is rather conflicting. Some reading surveys, such as those carried out in Brighton, Middlesbrough and Swansea, found girls superior to boys in reading ability; but the important carefully conducted Ministry of Education Reading Surveys of 1948, 1952 and 1956, (reported by Ministry of Education pamphlets dated 1950 and 1957) and Morris' (1966) recent survey found, if anything, that boys were superior to girls.

An interesting result was recorded when Thackray (1971) compared the mean reading scores of boys and girls in both his i.t.a. and t.o. groups separately. In the i.t.a. group there were no significant differences between the mean scores of the girls and the boys, but in the t.o. group significant differences between the mean scores of the boys and girls, in favour of the latter, were found throughout the three year investigation. This result suggests that with a simplified and regular medium such as i.t.a., boys should learn to read as easily as girls and the number of boy backward readers should be reduced. This is a problem well worth further investigation. However, taking Thackray's t.o. results separately, his evidence is in conflict with Morris's and agrees more with the American research results, i.e. girls tend to be somewhat superior to boys in early reading.

But is this difference between the reading achievements of girls and boys necessarily caused by physiological or maturational differences? The answer must be 'no'.

Nor is this conclusion weakened by the fact that American investigations and British research are completely in agreement with each other on the finding that many more boys than girls are found in special classes for disabled readers. In America, Monroe (1932) and Betts (1948), for example, both reported a higher incidence of boys as compared with girls attending reading clinics. In Britain also Schonell (1942) and Morris (1966) found more boys than girls were placed in special groups for backward readers. This does not even prove that boys are worse readers than girls. It only shows that boys are more likely to be *recognised* as poor readers by their teachers. Possibly, boys who are frustrated by reading failure react more violently than girls. Therefore, the boys' nuisance value would be higher and so they would get picked out and sent off to the special remedial reading treatment class more frequently than the girls, whose problem would be less noticeable. This is a tenable hypothesis.

We have kept to American and British research thus far because English is the language which both American and British children generally learn to read first (though not always, of course, e.g. Welsh). However, if we turn to research from other countries we find different results which force us to consider an alternative explanation of the differences in the reading attainments of girls and boys which have been found frequently in America and to some extent in Britain. For example, Viitaniemi (1965) examined sex differences in reading ability in schools in Finland. Boys obtained significantly superior achievements than girls on two comprehension tests, while girls were slightly but not significantly better in oral reading.

Abiri (1969) conducted a large-scale experiment on learning to read English in Nigeria. The pupils he studied were young beginners whose mother tongue was Yoruba. One group of classes was taught by i.t.a., while the other learned with t.o.

19

The i.t.a. medium proved superior, but what concerns us here is that in both groups, i.t.a. and t.o., the boys were superior to the girls. There is no reason to believe that the physiology of sex is different among the Yoruba people from what it is in American or British people. What differences other than physiological ones might give the boys the advantage in Nigeria? The most likely solution to this problem is the fact that girls have poorer school attendance records than boys in that country. This, in turn, is because, if some chore needs doing around the homestead, the girl is kept at home to do it, while the boy is allowed to go to school. But this apparently simple solution is actually a clue to an even more important factor in this situation, i.e. parental and social attitudes towards the different sexes.

In Nigeria, the girl may be kept at home to do the chores while the boy goes to school, because the parents value education more for their sons than for their daughters. If parental and social attitudes explain this difference between the reading achievements of boys as compared with girls in Nigeria, may not the same factor of social and parental attitudes explain the opposite difference in America?

In the American cultural pattern, parents usually have markedly different expectations of how their sons should behave and how their daughters ought to conduct themselves. These behaviour differences are not biologically or physiologically determined, but result from the cultural pressures represented in these parental expectations of what a boy should do and what a girl should do. For example, boys are expected and thereby encouraged to spend more time and energy on the large muscular activities, while girls are expected to and therefore do spend more time in sedentary activities. Even the language of girls is expected to be 'better' than that of boys, and that 'better' language is much more likely to be similar to the 'proper English' found in school reading books. If a pre-school girl spends a lot of time looking at books that behaviour would be very acceptable socially, but, if an American father sees his son with his nose in books to the same extent, he is more likely to think that his son ought to be doing something '*more boyish*' like running after a ball outside the house. Even when they enter school, boys who are very good at bookish activities have to be on their guard against being *too* good unless they are also good at physical games, otherwise their sexual role will be questioned by people calling them 'sissies'.

Another social factor which is concealed behind the apparent sex differences in·reading ability is the commonly held belief that the youngest pupils should be taught by women. This means that when a girl goes to school she can readily identify with her teacher who is a good reader and who wants her pupils to read like her. In contrast, the boy cannot so identify himself with his lady teacher. He has to be different. This socially determined discrimination against boys could well be sufficient to explain why American boys are less ready to learn to read than American girls. Gates (1961) found that the superiority of girls over boys appeared to be just as great in the upper grades of American schools as in the lower age levels. Therefore, he concludes that the North American social environment is such that 'more girls than boys pursue a kind of life in which more respect, more incentive, and more opportunities for reading appear earlier and persist longer'. Gates' conclusion has been supported by objective evidence from three recent studies: Downing and Thomson (in press), Dwyer (1973), and Johnson (1973).

Thus, we conclude that the differences between the reading ability of girls and that of boys found in most American and some British research, is not due to physiological sex differences. It is much more likely to be the effect of the different ways in which boys and girls are brought up and educated. In particular, parents seem to expect boys to engage in activities which are less likely to encourage readiness for reading. Also, the practice of employing women and not men in the youngest classes is a handicap for many boys.

The practical teacher, even if she is female, will bear in mind these socially-determined differences which make the boys less ready to receive her help in learning to read. She will find ways of showing the boys how reading and writing are important to *men* and in the things that men and boys like to do.

NEUROLOGICAL FACTORS

A very small proportion of children have chronic difficulty in learning to read in the early stages and this disability is sometimes attributed to neurological causes. This concept has been extended and it is sometimes suggested that a certain level of neurological development must be reached before any child is ready to learn to read.

The evidence for this view that there is an important neurological basis for reading readiness comes from studies either of brain-damaged patients or of children suffering from serious reading problems. Research on the former has been in the medical field, and in consequence the medical profession's preference for Greek or Latin terms has resulted in a number of such words spilling over into educational work on this problem. It is important for the teacher to understand that giving a

Greek or Latin label to the phenomenon of reading disability cannot by itself explain its cause. For example, 'dyslexia' is simply a Greek word meaning disturbance of reading. To say that 'reading disability is caused by dyslexia', therefore, may be quite meaningless. However, the concept of dyslexia also embraces the view that the disturbance of reading is caused by some defect in the brain.

Three other Greek words often occur in discussions of dyslexia. 'Dysgraphia' is the label for disturbance of writing. 'Aphasia' is the general term for the loss of speech or the ability to understand speech. 'Dysphasia' refers to a disturbance rather than a loss of speech. For example, a patient who has suffered brain damage following a stroke may still be able to speak, but he is not able reliably to say what he means. He may intend to tell his wife that he has just mowed the lawn, but say instead, 'I just cooked my hat.'

There is a very wide gap between the evidence for such conditions as aphasia and such hypothetical concepts as dyslexia. Aphasia is very well defined and firmly rooted in empirical evidence. The same cannot be said for 'dyslexia', as it is sometimes used in educational books and articles.

Medical research on brain-damaged patients, for example soldiers with bullet wounds in the brain, has established with certainty that such injuries cause loss or disturbance of language functions. Sometimes, such patients can make the necessary movements of the fingers and hands without any impairment, yet they can no longer write. This condition is also well established, and may appropriately be termed 'agraphia'. Similarly, brain-damaged patients who lose the ability to read may be said to be suffering from 'alexia'. Disturbed behaviour rather than complete loss of writing and reading as a result of *observed damage to the brain*, therefore, may be described quite appropriately as 'dysgraphia' and 'dyslexia'.

The first step away from this unequivocal fact of observation was taken when the term 'congenital aphasia' was proposed for cases where the patients exhibited the symptoms of aphasia, but had *no known factual history of physical injury to the brain*. Similarly, a step away from the certainty of observed cases of brain injury was taken when the term 'dyslexia' began to be applied to cases which exhibited the symptoms of disturbed reading but had *no known factual history of brain damage*. In the case of young children, a second step away from the original empirically based use of the terms is taken in applying the label 'dyslexia' to them because their disturbed reading behaviour is not the same as that in patients who are *no longer able* to read effectively. The so-called 'dyslexic' child *never has had that ability*. He or she has always been disturbed from the beginning.

A third step away from the established relationship between observed damage to the brain and loss or disturbance of one or more of the language abilities is in the theoretical proposal that such loss or damage can be associated with some specific part or area of the brain.

While it may seem feasible that language functions are localised in this way, it is extremely unlikely that reading would have a specific brain centre or cortical area. The development of writing and reading as universal phenomena in civilised societies is quite new, and it would be biologically impossible for such a specialised 'organ' to have been evolved in such a tiny segment of man's total history. Many primitive societies still have no writing and their people do not read. They can hardly be described as 'dyslexic'. This idea of a specific area of the brain which controls the function of reading seems to be a legacy of phrenology and faculty psychology, both of which have long since been discredited and discarded as scientific theories.

Yet, a number of authorities are convinced that a congenital brain defect, which they call 'dyslexia', is a real cause of failure to learn to read. They remain convinced that the similarity between the symptoms in such cases and those of patients where brain damage is known indicates a similar underlying brain defect. For example, Miles (1967) states that the 'basic justification for the concept of dyslexia is that it invites us to take the analogies with aphasia seriously.' The analogies which he refers to are in the symptoms of dyslexia of which he says the chief ones are:

1 'Persistent confusion over direction.' Especially reversals in reading (e.g. saying 'bog' for *dog*, or 'saw' for *was*), and in writing (e.g. 'dna' for *and*).

2 The inability to make sense of written marks. 'For dyslexic children . . . words are mere marks on paper.'

The latter symptom is often referred to as 'word-blindness', i.e. the child can see letters but he is 'blind' to their significance as words. He is unable to organise them meaningfully. Hinshelwood (1917) popularised this term for what he believed was a reading disability caused by a localised brain defect.

Witty and Kopel (1939) examined some other medical explanations of reading disability and found many of them bizarre, for example, inadequate blood and oxygen supply to certain brain centres, nervous exhaustion, a weakening of the excitability of the nervous tissue. In their summing up at that time Witty and Kopel state:

'Congenital word blindness for many years popularly regarded as a cause is still invoked by naïve persons to describe disability of which the causes are unknown. The concept has been demonstrated by neurologists and psychologists to be invalid.'

The evidence from the study of children who fail to learn to read is no more satisfactory than that from the medical field. For example, Schilder (1944) described seven cases of retarded reading, all of whom confused the letters *b* and *d*, etc. He seems to assume that this proves that a neurological defect causes the reversal, and that this in turn causes the reading disability, but he does not demonstrate this by his evidence. (We will return to the matter of reversals in the next section.) Another study typical of the evidence offered in support of this theory is that of Hallgren (1950). He compared 122 reading failure cases with 212 normal children, and reported that all but 13 of the children in the failure group had a family history of reading problems. His conclusion was that reading disability is due to some primary specific disability which these children had inherited from their families. But it is well known that such evidence contains a logical fallacy because families share also the same environment. Non-reading parents are not likely to provide the best environment for a child learning to read.

Many other examples of this weak type of evidence exist. When Russell Davis and Cashdan (1963) made a comprehensive review of all the evidence that had been offered, they were forced to conclude that the 'evidence has not yet been provided' for the existence of a neurologically based dyslexia.

Thus far, the evidence for the existence of a condition of neurological defect in dyslexia as a common cause of reading disability in children with no known history of brain damage is not at all convincing. Little wonder that Burt (1966) concludes:

'The neurologist no doubt has much to learn from the perplexing problem with which educationists are constantly confronted and especially from their correlational studies of individual differences; but there is little that the practical educationist can learn from the neurologist's somewhat speculative hypotheses fascinating though they are.'

He quotes a passage from Schonell with which he expresses agreement:

'Much harm has been done to remedying backwardness in reading by such cerebral theories as *word blindness*.'

There is, of course, no harm in theorising about dyslexia, and one would not want to discourage research on the neurological basis of reading disability. But, there may be harm in raising parents' hopes of a 'medical cure' for reading failure, and there may be harm in distracting or discouraging teachers from pursuing normal methods of remedial teaching, if dyslexia has been medically diagnosed.

Even if such a neurological basis for reading is valid, then the condition of dyslexia would seem likely to be a rare condition in the normal classroom, as is admitted by most authorities who hold the view that a neurologically based condition of dyslexia really exists. Both Harris (1961) and Vernon (1962) have recently pointed out that cases of specific dyslexia are rarely found in schools, although they may occur in clinics to which severe reading disability cases are referred. Other authorities who admit the possibility of dyslexia are Gesell and Amatruda (1941), and Jensen (1943). Both feel that there are cases of minimal birth injury which lead to an impairment of the ability to master language and reading, although there are no obviously physical handicaps noted.

Smith and Carrington (1959), suggest that in specific dyslexia there may be an inadequacy of brain functioning due to some biochemical peculiarity without any structural defect in brain tissue. They have attempted to explain all the different kinds of symptoms found in reading disabilities in terms of two chemicals which are probably involved in the conduction of nerve impulses in the brain. This explanation is an unproved hypothesis, but it does indicate the revival of interest in the possible validity of dyslexia during recent years.

Vernon (1962) puts forward the view that there does exist a number of cases who have great difficulty in learning to read which cannot be attributable to environmental or emotional factors. These, she considers, may possibly be cases of specific dyslexia, but she suggests that the neurological hypotheses are highly speculative and that the exact nature of the disability cannot be diagnosed without further and more accurate investigations. At the present time the controversy continues as to the reality of such a neurological condition as specific dyslexia.

This discussion has taken us rather a long way from the normal beginners in the everyday classroom with which this book is chiefly concerned. But this is because the evidence for a neurological state of readiness for reading is derived from such abnormal circumstances. This, in itself, leads to a further practical conclusion for the classroom teacher. Cases of neurological unreadiness seem likely to be very rare. Furthermore, the diagnosis of dyslexia is made by medical doctors, and, when it is made, the treatment, according to Miles, is 'kindness and encouragement on the part of the teacher.' As we would assume that kindness and encouragement is the usual treatment of all beginners, our conclusion is that, if any neurological factor in reading readiness exists, it is of no significance for classroom teaching methods.

CEREBRAL DOMINANCE, LATERALITY AND REVERSALS

Related to the neurological issues discussed in the previous section is the controversial issue of laterality and connected theories of cerebral dominance. Another kind of neurological condition of readiness for reading which has often been proposed is that children should have developed the neurological organization which is the basis for consistent preference for using the right hand and right eye, for example.

Lateral dominance refers to the use of one of the externally paired parts of the body (hands, eyes, feet). We are all aware that some people are right-handed, some are left-handed and some few are ambidextrous. A less commonly observed fact is that individuals also display a preference for the right or left eye when occasion demands, for example, looking through a telescope or a microscope. Sometimes an individual is dominant on one side for handedness and dominant on the other side for eyedness. This state of mixed dominance is termed 'crossed laterality'. Also, just as some people are ambidextrous, so they may equally well show no clear-cut preference for one eye rather than the other.

Burt (1937), Buswell (1937), MacMeeken (1939), Schonell (1940), and Monroe (1932), among others have studied the distribution of dominance in handedness and eyedness and also mixed dominance. The general consensus of their findings suggest that in any large unselected group of people, approximately 5 per cent are left-handed, 35 per cent are left-eyed, and 33 per cent have mixed dominance. The most plausible explanation as to why left-eyedness should occur so much more frequently than left-handedness is Burt's (1937) hypothesis of social conditioning. He postulates that right-handed people are more favoured than the left-handed, and as the hereditary disposition to handedness is slight, early social pressure which is brought to bear on the child to use his right hand succeeds in changing the disposition to left-handedness. In contrast, there is no social pressure for right-eyedness.

Theories incorporating cerebral dominance have been used to explain reading disability, the one most quoted in the literature being that of Orton (1929), a neurologist. He postulated that reversals in reading (such as 'was' for *saw*, 'top' for *pot*, 'on' for *no*) found very frequently in cases of reading disability

26

and in children just beginning to read, resulted from uncertainty of orientation, sometimes called directional confusion, which in turn was due to lack of clearly established dominance in one hemisphere of the brain. Orton assumed that the ability to perceive and recognise visual stimuli is a function of identical areas in both hemispheres of the brain, but the ability to recognise a word requires the operation of one of these areas, in one hemisphere only. He postulated that the right-sided person develops memory traces for printed words in a part of the left hemisphere, but also in the right hemisphere, the less active centre, and these are mirror images of those on the dominant side. When the clearly right- or clearly left-sided person reads, only the memory traces on the dominant side are aroused; difficulty in reading occurs when unilateral dominance is not clearly established. In such cases, according to Orton, the child will have great difficulty in learning to read and spell, and reversal errors will be prevalent.

Orton's theory has become less plausible as neurological science has developed and more has been learned about the brain and central nervous system. For example, eyedness cannot be an indication of the dominance of one cerebral hemisphere because both eyes are represented in both hemispheres.

Another theory of laterality in relation to reading is that of Dearborn (1933). He proposed that the easiest and most natural bodily movements are away from the centre of the body, and so right-handed persons make movements from left to right more easily than those from right to left; similarly it is easier for a right-eyed person to look from left to right than in the opposite direction. Conversely, left-handed and left-eyed persons will find right to left movements easier, and more natural than movements from left to right. But in the English language, reading and writing is from left to right, and Dearborn feels that children with left-handed or left-eyed dominance, and particularly children with mixed dominance, may experience difficulty in following from left to right.

Both Orton's and Dearborn's theories are affected by the research evidence on (1) mixed dominance and (2) reversals in reading failure.

1 *Mixed dominance*
The evidence on the relationship between mixed dominance and reading disability is conflicting. Harris (1961) and Schonell (1940) both found a positive connection between them, i.e., reading disability cases more frequently showed mixed dominance. But the researches of Woody and Phillips (1934) and Wittenborn (1946) reversed this conclusion. Other studies of

this problem include those by Teegarden (1932), Davidson (1934), Hildreth (1934), Frank (1935), Witty and Kopel (1939), Monroe (1932), Gates (1949), Kennedy (1954), and Furness (1956). Their consensus indicated that handedness is not significantly related to reading ability, but that mixed hand-eye dominance is slightly related. However, two more recent investigations, Belmont and Birch (1963) and Rosenberger (1967), failed to find any significant increase in the incidence of incomplete or crosed laterality in poor as compared with good readers. Regarding eyedness alone and reading ability the evidence is contradictory.

Hildreth (1950) reviewed all the research evidence and concluded that there is no evidence for a causal connection between handedness and speech or reading defects. However, Harris (1961) remains convinced that there is a connection. He believes that the conflict of evidence is due to the use of insensitive tests of laterality in some of the investigations. In 1957 Harris reported a new study in which he found twice as many mixed dominance cases in his reading disability group as compared with a group of normal readers.

The most recent research on this problem is the new Scottish study by Clark (1967). She reports that the incidence of left-handedness in handwriting is increasing due to greater tolerance on the part of teachers and parents. About 8 per cent of Scottish children write with the left hand as compared with 5 per cent in earlier research. About one third of the children in 1967 were left-eyed, which shows no increase over previous studies. This is further confirmation of Burt's social conditioning hypothesis. Clark points out that crossed laterality must be very common in the population:

'A considerable proportion of children must have their preferred hand and eye on opposite sides. Even if one were to assume that every left-handed child were left-eyed (which is not the case), at least one quarter of the children would be crossed laterals. It is important when considering the significance, if any, of crossed laterality that it be appreciated just how common a phenomenon it is.'

It is generally agreed that the hypothesis that confused brain dominance is the cause of reading difficulties is too speculative to have any practical value at present. Consequently, the beginning reading teacher can obtain no effective estimate of a child's readiness for learning to read from any test of handedness or eyedness.

One other theory of brain dominance and neurological readiness should be mentioned. Delacato (1963) believes that there is a definite sequence of stages of neurological organisation through which a child must proceed if he is to be ready to learn to read successfully. If this normal sequence of development is interrupted it causes difficulties both in mobility and in language learning—especially reading. At the highest level of development described by Delacato, one finds clear dominance of feet, hands, and eyes. In contrast mixed laterality is evidence of poor neurological organisation. High musical ability is associated with crossed laterality, according to Delacato. At the 'cortical level' of development the child *walks* with good balance, smoothly, in a cross-patterned manner (e.g. right arm balancing left leg, etc.). Tracing the developmental sequence backwards to the next stage, we find the 'midbrain level', at which the child shows smooth, rhythmical cross-pattern *creeping*. At the lowest level, the *pons* level, the child has a good *sleeping position* appropriate to his laterality. If this sequence has been interrupted it should be corrected by finding where it occurred, and retraining the child from that point onwards.

Delacato reports a series of experiments of his own which he claims support his theory through the success of the treatment described above. As a result quite a few American schools are treating reading disability by having children crawl round the gymnasium. It is rumoured that some schools have debated whether to give up teaching music because of its hypothesised connection with crossed laterality.

Enough has been said already about the lack of evidence in support of any causal relationship between crossed laterality and reading falure, but this should be remembered again when considering Delacato's theory that there is a neurological organisation factor in reading readiness. Furthermore, Delacato's claims have been subjected to careful scrutiny by Glass and Robins (1967). They describe Delacato's statements as 'extravagant claims for validity', and of his experiments they comment, 'without exception, these experiments contained major faults in design and analysis.'

2 *Reversals*

A connection between reversals and reading disability has been claimed as evidence in support of theories of dyslexia (Schilder), and mixed dominance (Orton, Dearborn). For example, Orton regarded reversals in reading and writing as symptoms of a more general tendency of 'strephosymbolia', which is also displayed by children who are confused about putting their clothes on the right way round, or who cannot find their way home by remembering the direction to follow. Also, a number of other research workers who have not followed these particular theories have felt that there may be a causal connection between reversals and reading failure. For instance, Monroe (1932), Tinker (1934), and Harris (1961) all found more reversal tendencies in retarded readers than in normal readers. This seems to have led to the belief that, if a child reverses words like *saw* and *was*, or *on* and *no*, or letters like *b* and *d*, or *n* and *u*, it is an indication of immaturity of perceptual development, i.e., the child is not ready to learn to read because his perceptual development has not progressed far enough for him to be able to distinguish between the alternative directions of such reversible symbols.

However, Lynn (1963) cites an experiment by Newson in 1955 which demonstrated that four- to four-and-a-half-year-olds could discriminate such mirror images better after thirty minutes' training than five-year-olds who received no special training, from which Newson concluded that 'The existence of this disability at five must be taken as being due entirely to lack of experience in the practice of this concept.'

Actually, the tendency to confuse *d* and *b*, *n* and *u*, etc. is more likely to be due to *good* perceptual development rather than the opposite because the child's experiences prior to coming to school will have taught him to ignore such mirror images. He has learned the lesson well that a walking stick is still 'a stick' no matter in which direction the handle is pointing. When he learns to read he must learn that in reading and writing the direction *does matter*. The letters *b* and *d* are not both sticks with a handle. The one pointing to the left represents one sound while the one pointing to the right means something different.

The retarded reader who continues to make reversals has failed to unlearn the generalisation he had learned before coming to school. Thus it is much more likely that reversals are a symptom of reading failure than its cause. Hence, we conclude that the tendency to reverse letters and words in the beginning stage is quite normal and cannot be regarded as any indication of lack of readiness to learn to read or write.

In summary, the classroom teacher who wishes to judge a child's readiness for reading can obtain no practical help from a consideration of possible neurological factors as evidenced by such tendencies as crossed laterality, or reversals.

VISION, HEARING AND SPEECH

Vision

Some of the earlier studies in the field of reading investigated the relation between visual defects and reading performance as it was supposed that the cause of poor reading could be traced to some kind of visual defect. However, although a large number of studies have been carried out in this field, both by oculists and psychologists, the results reported have varied widely, and an exact statement of the degree to which poor reading is caused by poor vision still cannot be made.

Witty and Kopel (1936a, b and c), Swanson and Tiffen (1936), Dalton (1943), Monroe (1932), and Edson, Bond and Cook (1953), among others, found little or no relationship between visual defects and reading ability. On the other hand some investigators, such as Eames (1938), Park and Burri (1943), and Robinson (1946), have found evidence of a relationship between certain types of visual defects and reading failures; they place more emphasis on such visual difficulties as poor near-point acuity, and poor eye muscle balance with accompanying deficiency in fusion and depth perception. Turning to the more direct concern with the readiness of the eye for the reading task all investigators feel that it is important to make an early check on children's vision and to keep close watch on their progress in the early stages of reading.

On the question of the typical age at which the child's eyes are developed sufficiently for reading with them, there is, even in this rather obviously practical matter, a conflict of opinion. Jacques, an optometrist, is reported by Witty and Koppel (1936a and b) to have declared that the eyes are not mature enough before the age of eight. But Shaw (1964), an ophthalmologist, believes that the eyes are sufficiently well developed to handle the task of reading already by the age of twelve months.

What is an agreed fact is that children are born farsighted, and that, as the eyeball lengthens, it becomes adapted for near vision. Jacques's view is that it is not certain that this adaptation has progressed far enough before the age of eight years, wheras Shaw believes that it has adapted enough for effective reading by the end of the first year of life. The careful teacher's viewpoint is reflected by Cole (1938), who prefers to wait until the child is aged eight years, rather than run the risk of either damaging the child's self-confidence or, possibly, his eyes.

The fear that too early a start in reading may injure the eyes has been expressed by other writers. Leverett (1957) conducted research on the incidence of myopia in children at age levels between five and seventeen. He found the older the age group the greater was the incidence of myopia. Kosinski (1957) believes that myopia is a symptom of a general weakness of connective tissue which may be caused by the eye movements made in reading.

The evidence of all these problems of the readiness of the eyes for reading tasks remains inconclusive. But as Holmes (1968) concludes in his review of research, there is sufficient evidence to maintain doubts about the effects of early reading on the development of the eyes and, therefore, to warrant more research on this problem. From the point of view of the practical question of judging when a child's eyes are ready for the task of reading, it would seem that the eyes of a normal child are ready for this task at the usual age of beginning school, but that the teacher should watch carefully for signs of visual discomfort. Referral to the competent professional eye specialist should be made if some visual defect is suspected, and the specialist's recommendations should be followed, e.g. glasses worn, or the child seated appropriately for reading.

Hearing

Most teachers recognise easily the distinction between the sensation of vision on the one hand and visual perception on the other. In the previous section we have quite clearly been concerned merely with visual sensation. Visual perception which is concerned with the *interpretation* of what is sensed by the eye is the province of Chapter 5. Similarly, in this section on 'hearing' we shall deal only with auditory acuity and not auditory discrimination or perception. By 'auditory acuity' we refer to the ability to use the ears to sense auditory stimuli. 'Auditory discrimination' is a technical term used to describe the child's ability to perceive the phonemes (sounds) of which words are composed. This also is discussed in Chapter 5.

According to Burton (1956), a person with normal auditory acuity can, (*a*) hear sounds covering a considerable range of sound wave frequencies, (*b*) distinguish between sounds of different frequencies or pitch, and (*c*) can blend, or fuse, sounds effectively through the use of both ears. Impaired hearing could create difficulties in reading. A child with subnormal hearing does not receive a clear presentation of sounds to copy and so frequently mis-pronounces words he speaks; again he finds difficulty in correcting his pronunciation errors as he has an inadequate auditory check on his own sounds.

However, although a hearing impairment may be a factor relating to poor reading in an individual case, the researches of Bond (1935), and Gates and Bond (1936), into the relationship between auditory acuity and reading performance give no clear evidence that groups of poor readers are inferior in auditory capacity to groups of normal readers and some researchers, such as those of Witty and Kopel (1939), Kennedy (1942), and

Robinson and Hall (1942), show a negative relationship.

But one type of hearing impairment was found to be a cause of reading difficulty in several studies. Robinson is one of several researchers who have found that high frequency hearing loss was consistently associated with reading failure. This condition results in poor acuity for sounds of high frequency or pitch. The effect is to make it difficult for the child suffering from this condition to hear sounds like those heard at the beginning of words like *sigh, fie, thigh.*

Witty and Kopel, and Bond both make the point that the effects of hearing handicap on progress in learning to read may depend on the methods of teaching. For example, methods which emphasise the phonic aspect of learning to read are less likely to succeed with children who suffer from defects in hearing.

It would appear from the research that, given a degree of hearing sufficient to enable the child to join in the activities of the ordinary classrom, then auditory acuity is not closely related to success in reading. From the point of view of reading readiness, the main general conclusion for educational practice is that children should be examined expertly for defects in their auditory abilities when they enter school, or before they start to read. By far the most satisfactory way to measure hearing is to use an audiometer, but the whisper and the watch-tick tests are reasonably satisfactory ones.

Speech

Children who find difficulty in speaking often find difficulty in learning to read as speech impediments affect reading in several ways, the most common of them being stuttering, lisping, slurring and generally indistinct speech. Again children who cannot speak clearly usually find phonetic analysis difficult. Research into the relationship between speech defects and reading achievement is very limited and typical researches are those of Bond (1935), Bennett (1938), Gaines (1941), Monroe (1932), Gates (1949) and Robinson and Hall (1942). What research there is does indicate a definite connection, but there is insufficient evidence to claim a causal relationship. Although the cause is not understood, the evidence is quite clear that children with speech problems such as lisping and stuttering do frequently have difficulties in learning to read. If the teacher detects such problems, the child should be referred to the speech therapist for specialist treatment as early as possible.

Returning to the general theme of these several chapters on physiological factors in readiness, the general conclusion to be drawn is that this area seems a relatively unimportant one for classroom teaching practices, provided that children are examined expertly for physical defects and particularly those of vision, hearing and speech, when they enter school, and that the prescriptions of such clinical specialists are followed.

Chapter 3 Enviromental Factors

SOCIO-ECONOMIC AND OTHER ENVIRONMENTAL FACTORS

The cultural background of the home has been found to bear a relationship to reading readiness and reading progress. This broad group of factors, often referred to as 'home background', includes a number of environmental aspects, some more important than others, but all affecting the total experience the child brings to the reading situation.

Schonell (1961) suggests that 'home background' includes the following:

1 Economic conditions, such as relate to income of the family, size of house, sufficiency and regularity of meals and sleep, etc.;

2 Opportunity for play and for social experiences of different kinds—these, of course, are linked with growth of concepts and vocabulary (see also Chapter 5);

3 Nature and amount of speech and language patterns of children, particularly as they are influenced by the talk of their parents (see Chapter 3);

4 Attitudes towards reading and writing, the amount of reading done in the home, and the availability of books of varying levels of difficulty;

5 Quality of family life in terms of inter-parental relationships, as they influence the child's security and personality growth generally.

Such aspects of the home background determine the quality of the experience the child brings to the reading situation, and experience is a basic pre-requisite for reading. Our definition of reading includes the gaining of meaning from printed symbols. Meaning comes from the mind of the reader who gives to these symbols meaningful ideas based on his own past experience.

Research on these aspects of home background seems to have been chiefly of three kinds: (i) studies of the relationship between *socio-economic* class levels and reading progress; (ii) investigations of *specific qualities of children's homes* and their success in beginning reading; and (iii) research on the *'cultures'* to which children belong and their influence on learning to read. We will examine all of these in this chapter.

When research workers have confined themselves simply to the investigation of socio-economic class as such only a slight or negligible relationship with reading progress has been found. For example Anderson and Kelly (1931), in their comparative study of 100 poor readers and 100 normal readers matched for age, sex and intelligence, were unable to find any significant differences between the groups, with regard to the father's occupation, the general economic status of the home, the occurrence of 'broken homes', or the general emotional atmosphere prevalent in the home. Similar evidence can be found in the studies of Bennett (1938), Ladd (1933) and Fleming (1943). For example, Fleming found the correlation between reading performance and socio-economic class was in the order of ·3. But so also was the correlation between reading performance and I.Q. Therefore, there was no evidence that differences in reading ability are directly caused by differences of socio-economic class. Other studies have shown similar results, e.g., Gesell and Lord (1927), Peck and McGlothlin (1940).

Those studies which have investigated the comparative richness of experience available to children in different homes rather than their simple socio-economic status have shown the importance of the former on the development of the child's reading ability. A valuable study to illustrate this point is the one made by Hilliard and Troxell (1937). They investigated the relationship between rich, or meagre backgrounds of experience at home and success in reading, by using seventy kindergarten children and following their reading progress to the second grade. At the beginning of the experiment Hilliard and Troxell gathered all possible information concerning each child's pre-school and present environment and background, e.g., availability of good picture books, good speech, interesting ideas, etc. The children's I.Q.s were determined and then they were divided into two groups, one group with meagre background of home experiences, the other with rich backgrounds. Reading tests were given to both groups at the end of six months in the first grade, and again at the end of four months in the second grade. It was found that the group with rich background experiences at home was two months ahead of the poor group at the initial testing, and six months ahead at the second testing.

Many other studies, such as those of Hildreth (1933), Witty and Kopel (1939), Sheldon and Carrillo (1952), in America, and those of Burt (1937), McClelland (1942), Schonell (1942), Fleming (1943), McClaren (1950), and Morris (1966) in Britain, lend support to the findings of Hilliard and Troxell. These studies all found a positive relationship between children's experiential backgrounds at home and reading progress.

The conclusion from the studies reviewed in this chapter is that socio-economic class is related to reading readiness, but that this is not a direct causal relationship. We may anticipate that children from lower socio-economic class homes may tend to be ready for reading somewhat later than those from others, but this is due simply to the fact that certain types of experiences are *less likely* to be available to individual children in poorer homes. Books and other forms of written language are *less likely* to be in evidence. Parental attitudes are *less likely* to be positive towards intellectual activities such as reading. Parents are *less likely* to read to their children. Parents are *less likely* to hold elaborate conversations with them. We have emphasised that it is only 'less likely' because there is tremendous overlap between the socio-economic classes in all these studies. A teacher should never be fatalistic about the chances of her pupils who come from lower socio-economic status homes. Rather, she should be prepared for differences between her own home background and that of her pupils, and optimistic about the outcome of adjusting to the needs of these children. Many of them *do* become excellent readers, despite their original lack of those advantages which have a greater probability (but, again, no certainty) of occurring in the homes of children in the higher socio-economic levels. Similarly, the conclusion from the parents' point of view is the same no matter how they may feel themselves to be classified economically or socially. Their children need richness of experience especially in language, and that costs parental time rather than money. The investment of time in talking with children and sharing the content of books with children is probably the most certain method of helping them to get ready for learning to read. This applies both at school as well as at home.

CULTURAL FACTORS

The 1960s in America saw a rapidly increasing interest in 'cultural' factors in reading progress. Downing's (1968) paper on this topic at the *Third International Reading Symposium* at the University of Southampton, and his evidence to the Plowden Commission (Central Advisory Council for Education, 1967) on the same subject were typical of the spread of interest in this problem to educators in Britain. The Plowden suggestions regarding 'priority areas' grew out of this growing concern for those children who are termed 'culturally disadvantaged'.

Some people have misunderstood this term. The word 'culture' in this context has that special technical meaning given to it in the sciences of sociology and anthropology. It refers to the total way of life of a relatively homogeneous group of people. For example, we can contrast English culture with, say, Italian culture, and we do not refer only to such differences as exist between the operas of Benjamin Britten and Rossini, or the art of Constable and Da Vinci. In this technical use of 'culture', we would include all other aspects of the ways of life of the English as compared with the Italians, e.g., how they toilet train their babies, how they drive their cars, their marriage customs, their languages, etc. Clearly, both English culture and Italian culture are 'good'. Neither can be said to be 'more cultured' than the other. To make such a claim would be to misuse this valuable objective concept from the social sciences.

Within cultures there exist 'sub-cultures'. For example, within the English culture we can discern the sub-cultural patterns of life of say Yorkshiremen and Devonians. Again, we cannot say that one sub-culture is better than the other. Each sub-culture is 'just right' for the people who belong to it. We can only say, if we are objective and fair to both, that they are *different*.

Now, social classes too are recognised as constituting sub-cultures. For example, Spinley (1953) made a scientific study of how personality grows differently as a result of the child's different experiences in the upper-class sub-culture and the working-class sub-culture. Again, if we are to remain objective and unprejudiced, we cannot condemn either of these sub-cultures. We cannot say that the working-class sub-culture is not as good as that of the upper-class or *vice versa*. Nor can we say that the upper-class man is 'more cultured' than the working-class man. To do so is simply to make a prejudiced value judgement. The working-class member is really just as cultured as any other as far as his own cultural values are concerned.

However, there are certain 'facts of life' which the teacher is forced to recognise in her treatment of children in her classroom who may be culturally different from herself. For example, an upper-class English accent has prestige, a middle-class pronunciation is acceptable, but some working-class accents are regarded as 'bad' by employers and other people in positions of power and authority. Thus a working-class child may be not only culturally different but also 'culturally disadvantaged' because the sub-culture his parents have given him in his upbringing just does not happen to be the one which is approved by the larger culture. In particular, his teachers and the whole educational system is geared to a different sub-culture from the one which he has naturally accepted as good – good for his parents, good for his brothers and sisters, good for his friends and therefore, good for him.

In this social problem of the culturally disadvantaged, we find the most glaring examples of the way in which the child's home background can make a child either more ready or less ready for learning to read. This problem has been expressed succinctly in the report of the Task Force of the (American) National Council of Teachers of English (1965) as follows:

'What an urban disadvantaged child does have are *experiences different from those which are expected in school.*'

Deutsch's (1960) description of his research on this problem of the negro child in New York City brings out the importance of cultural factors in readiness in all its stark reality.

'School is an experience which . . . is discontinuous with the values, preparation and experience they receive from their homes and particular community; it represents society's demand that they bridge social class orientations for a few hours a day, five days a week. No catalyst is provided for this transition and few plans have been made to facilitate the child's daily journey across the chasm.'

Reading may be valued highly in the sub-culture to which most teachers belong, but this judgement is reversed in some other sub-cultures. Bloom, Davis and Hess (1965) explain:

'The roots of their problem may in large part be traced to their experiences in homes which do not transmit the cultural patterns necessary for the types of learning characteristic of the schools and the larger society.'

The result is not simple stagnation or retardation. This cultural unreadiness for school is cumulative in its effect, as Corbin (1965) has pointed out:

'The standard curriculum to which they are committed hastens the decay of their egos and reduces, rather than strengthens, their ability to deal successfully with books, ideas, and language. Instead of growing, their measured I.Q.'s decline as they advance from grade to grade, though we know in general that growth is the normal pattern of the human intellect.'

This tendency for I.Q.s to be depressed through such experiences of conflict between the sub-culture of the home and that of school is certainly suggested by the results of a number of research investigations, e.g., Gordon (1924), Asher (1935),

Edwards and Jones (1938), Newman, Freeman, and Holzinger (1937), Neff (1928), Lee (1951), Kirk (1965).

The heart of the problem of the conflict between the two sub-cultures of home and school lies in the teacher's expectations of *what the child should be ready to learn* in reading. It is also another face of the basic problem of reading readiness — i.e., *readiness to read WHAT? What content? What language?* For example, until quite recently, all children in California had to take their first lessons in reading in English. It was assumed that a child who was ready for reading was ready for reading *English.* The result was that many children from *Spanish* speaking homes became chronic reading disability cases. Recent reforms have made it possible for them to learn reading first in Spanish and then, a little later, in English — with much greater success. This has an important object lesson. The child who is ready to learn to read is ready to relate *his experiences* to the new language medium of print or writing. But what exactly are *his experiences?* The Spanish-speaking child's experiences are of the Spanish language, and so he is ready to learn to read Spanish — but not English.

Now, the same logically must be true of cultural or sub-cultural differences in language. As the National Council of Teachers of English Task Force's report states:

'Most disadvantaged children come from homes in which a non-standard English dialect is spoken.'

Some people make the error of interpreting this as evidence of a linguistic vacuum.

For example, Pitman and St John (1969) have suggested that children who are not capable of benefiting from the Initial Teaching Alphabet (i.t.a.) in the first year of school are unready for it because of a deficiency in 'linguistic competence'. But these authors are judging from the limited point of view of their own upper-class sub-culture. The truth is that working-class children are highly competent in *their* language even if it is not recognised as 'real language' by such authors. Goodman's (1969) psycholinguistic analysis of the problem is much more convincing:

'Every child brings to school, when he comes, five or six years of language and of experience.

'In every respect the process of language development of the divergent speaker is exactly the same as that of the standard speaker. His language when he enters school is just as systematic, just as grammatical within the norms of his dialect, just as much a part of him as any other child's is.

'If the teacher "corrects" the dialect-based divergent language, this is at cross purposes wth the direction of growth of the child. All his past and present language experience contradicts what the teacher tells him. School becomes a place where people talk funny and teachers tell you things about your language that aren't true.'

Furthermore, if the child's dialect is characterized as 'bad' or 'not good' English, his past experiences of his own family and home are made worthless. As Goodman points out: 'His best defence is to be silent.' Then he may be diagnosed as suffering from a lack of the 'linguistic competence' of Pitman and St John. The extreme naivety of such a judgement of a child's *language* serves to remind us again of the need in considering reading readiness to have constantly before us the question 'ready for *exactly what* kind of reading activity?' In this case— 'reading *whose* language; the child's or the teachers?'

Loban (1965) clearly recognizes the need for teachers to adapt their language expectations more towards the child's own patterns of linguistic behaviour:

'Now we face a critical problem: the children speak a social class dialect. In the kindergarten and in the earliest years of school, the emphasis should be upon the child's using *whatever dialect of the language he already speaks* as the means of thinking and exploring and imagining. We need teachers who know that such dialects are essentially respectable and good.'

If we extend Loban's statement to apply it specifically to readiness for reading, we can see that a child with a good foundation of experience, say, in the Cockney dialect, is ready for reading in terms of those Cockney dialect experiences, but probably not in the so-called standard English dialect of his teacher.

Yet the usual procedure is to force the Cockney child to learn the printed form for the teacher's dialect—not the child's own. The resulting conflict is much deeper than just a confused mismatch of two dialects. Language is the holy of holys of culture. Therefore, to attack an individual's language is to commit an act of sacrilege on his culture. No wonder that the reaction is hostile, albeit coldly or dumbly so. As Corbin (1965) has described it:

'The perceptive teacher ... discovers ... that he and his pupils do not speak the same language and, furthermore, that they see very little reason for adopting his. Their families, their street mates, after all, speak theirs, not his.'

Tax (1965) comments:

'They often *cannot* do what the teacher asks, things which seem to them, consciously or unconsciously to denigrate their homes, their people, and their culture.'

Does this mean that we should provide children with beginning reading material in their own dialect? Goodman recognises that is one possibility to be considered, i.e., 'to write materials for them that are based on their own dialect.' However, he doubts its feasibility on several counts:

'Primarily the opposition of parents and leaders in the speech community must be reckoned with. They would reject the use of special materials which are based on a non-prestigious dialect.'

But Goodman may be overly pessimistic about such opposition. Wolfram and Fasold (1969), in considering the same dialect, i.e., Black English in America, come to the opposite conclusion:

'If a realisation develops that this dialect, an important part of black culture, is as distinctively Afro-American as anything in the culture, the result may well be a new respect for Black English within the community.'

Stewart (1969) also sees this as a really practical way of adapting the learning task to the dialect speaker's readiness for reading in his own dialect:

'Instead of being ignored or made the target of an eradication programme, Negro dialect should actually be used as a basis for teaching oral and written standard English. If Negro dialect is used to teach initial word-reading skills to Negro-dialect speakers, then those word-reading skills can be made the constant in terms of which standard-English grammatical patterns can be taught through reading and writing.'

British teachers, too, can consider the same approach to the problems of teaching reading to some of the sub-cultures represented in their classrooms, e.g., Cockneys, West Indian immigrants, etc. This is a way of narrowing the gap between the child's readiness level and the level of difficulty he faces in the learning task. He may be quite unready to learn to read in someone else's dialect (i.e., the teacher's) yet perfectly ready to develop skill in the basic processes of reading when the passages to be read are given to him in his own dialect.

Goodman (1970) states bluntly, 'Where it is at all feasible the child should achieve initial literacy within his own language (in fact within his own home dialect).' Research testing such dialect-based reading materials is currently under way in Washington, D.C. The results promise to throw light on fascinating theoretical issues and vital practical problems for an important section of the community, not only in America but also in Britain and many other countries.

Meanwhile, there are certain practical steps which can be taken without delay to adapt the reading task more to the child's level of readiness in respect of language. Home-made books, charts, etc. are clearly more likely to be closer to the child's own experience than any which a publisher can produce. Therefore, the 'Language-Experience Approach' to reading, as it is termed by Allen (1961), is more likely to come closer to the young beginner's need for reading related to his own background, than mass-produced basal reading schemes.

But publishers too can learn from these recent developments in the linguistics and psychology of cultural and sub-cultural differences. Indeed it is doubtful if any human being ever utters the weird jargon sometimes found in basic readers. Children do not say, 'This is a house. This is a man. The man is in the house.' As a *minimal* attempt to fit the basic reader's language to the child's, they could change the style to 'That's a house and that's a man. He's in the house.'

But there is another important aspect of this need to bridge the gap between the child's past and current experiences outside school and the demands of learning to read. That is in the *content* of what has to be read. The reading material needs to be close to the child's own experience, not only of language but of the life the language describes.

Several writers have shown how the culturally disadvantaged child is *made to be unready for reading by the reading materials we give him to read*. The following quotations make this point:

Whipple (1966):
'Children learn to read best when they can identify with the environment, the characters and situations presented in their readers. The typical reader with its all-white characters and suburban settings and activities does not give culturally-deprived children a sense of belonging, a feeling of security.'

Deutsch (1960):
'For example, an early grade primer presents country situations, and yet the vast majority of these children have never been to the country. Similarly, the primers are not bi-racial, and often have meaningless story content, and fail to present situations with which these children can become involved, or to picture children with whom they can identify. Instead of making school

a more meaningful experience for these children who most need it, such instructional materials serve only to turn to them another of society's unsmiling faces.'

National Council of Teachers of English Task Force (1965): 'Showing a picture of a white policeman with the caption "The policeman is my friend" may draw a reaction from the Negro children in Harlem or in Philadelphia, Missouri, quite different from that naturally expected by a middle-class white teacher.'

This last quoted comment is only an extreme example of this problem of making the content of the reading material fit the child's level of readiness in respect of his cultural background and experiences. Blom and Wiberg recently made a scientific study of the relationships between culture and children's reading books. They found a clear connection between cultural values and reading materials. These results form part of Downing's (1973) *Comparative Reading*, a comprehensive investigation of reading in different countries of the world and their varying languages.

The practical implications regarding the content of children's early reading are similar to those in respect of language and dialect. The language-experience approach is the teaching method most likely to insure that the content of children's reading matches their own experience. When children and teachers make up their own books they are much more likely to reflect the real-life activities of the children's own environment and culture as well as their own language than the mass-produced books of any publisher.

In this chapter we have found an area of real importance for reading readiness. The child's home background and his culture or sub-culture especially are extremely significant determinants of readiness. In this discussion we have also come closer to the teacher's approach to reading readiness which is most likely to be effective in the classroom. Readiness is only a relative concept. What the child must be ready for is not some fixed and unchangeable task of 'reading'. We can modify our 'reading' demands according to the individual pupil's level of readiness. *The teacher must give the child the kind of reading activity which he individually is ready for.* In terms of home background and culture, this means providing activities which involve reading (and writing) about the child's own home background and the child's own cultural and sub-cultural experiences. Moreover, the language to be read should be the printed or written form of the language or dialect the pupil knows already.

Chapter 4 Emotional Factors

EMOTIONAL AND PERSONALITY FACTORS

Nearly all investigators of these factors agree that emotional disturbances and personality difficulties do appear frequently where there is difficulty in learning to read. For example in one investigation Gates (1936) drew up a list of different symptoms of emotional and personality maladjustment in 100 cases of children having difficulty in reading. The most usual symptoms were the following:

1 extreme self-consciousness; easily hurt, blushes readily, has curious and egocentric manners, inferior feelings.

2 inclination to submissiveness, indifferent, inattentive, seemingly lazy.

3 withdrawn; day-dreaming, evasive reactions, joins gangs, plays truant, withdraws from society.

4 nervous tension and habitual nervous actions such as nail-biting, restlessness, stammering, sleeplessness.

But which was the cause and which was the effect? Did the emotional and personality disorders cause the reading disability or did the experience of failure and frustration in being unable to read cause the personality problems and emotional disturbances? This is a well-known 'chicken and egg' question in the study of reading disability.

Some investigators have hypothesised that emotional disturbances precede and cause difficulties in reading, or that such reading difficulties are one of the symptoms of a fundamentally inadequate personality adjustment. The following list of possible causes of emotional disturbances that may precede reading difficulties is adapted from Monroe (1935b):

1 over-protection from parents, most often by the mother. A child who is kept unduly dependent upon adults may feel that learning to read is an impossible task to undertake alone.

2 faulty training in the home. A child accustomed to unwise training methods, to inconsistent and unpredictable occurrences at home, may find it very difficult to make adjustments to the authoritative direction and systematic order of affairs at school.

3 unfair pressure by adults. A child who is urged to read before he is ready, to read materials beyond his ability, to do as well as a brother, or a sister, may develop feelings of defeatism,

resentment or antagonism, that prevent him from making normal reading progress.

The investigations of Bird (1927), Blanchard (1928), Robinson (1946), Young and Gaier (1951), among others, provide evidence which indicates that difficulties in learning to read can be a result of emotional and personal difficulties.

On the other hand Monroe (1932), maintains that personality difficulties and emotional problems are more frequently the results, rather than the causes, of reading disabilities, and Schonell (1961) arrived at the same conclusion. He writes:

'It is, however, from the mental effects of failure that most emotional difficulties arise. The sense of failure before companions, teachers and parents, weighs heavily upon pupils and in time, not only undermines self-confidence and self-esteem but breeds an apathy and disatisfaction that causes the child to run away from reading to seek success elsewhere.'

It becomes apparent that while the majority of the investigators who have studied the relationship between emotional and personality difficulties and reading disability agree that they are frequently found together, they disagree as to which is cause and which effect. Gates (1941) reviewed the evidence available on this issue and came to the conclusion that approximately 75 per cent of the more severe cases of reading disability which were referred to clinics showed some degree of maladjustment, and that in one quarter of such cases the maladjustment had caused the reading failure, while in three-quarters of cases the maladjustment was the accompaniment or the result of failure in learning to read.

It must be borne in mind that, in any case, the incidence of severe reading disability cases in which emotional disorders occur is quite a small fraction of the total population. Thus the number of children a teacher is likely to meet who are unready for reading because of emotional or personality disorder is extremely small. Dechant (1970) recommends, 'The teacher must be slow in attributing the reading difficulties of even one child to emotional and/or social problems.' If a child is showing signs of both reading failure and emotional disorder, then Dechant states:

'The first assumption that should be made is that the emotional disturbances are the result, rather than the cause of reading failure. One of the great rationalisations in the classroom for doing nothing or giving up is that the child is emotionally disturbed.'

If the teacher does come across a real case of emotional or personality disorder, the school's responsibility is to suggest a visit to the Educational Psychologist at the Child Guidance Centre. But this will rarely be necessary. More frequently, following Dechant's advice, she will assume that the child is upset because of failure and frustration in the overly difficult reading tasks she is asking the pupil to perform. The child who is emotionally disturbed about reading is most likely one who has been pressed to go too fast beyond his level of readiness intellectually (as we shall see in Chapter 5). In plain language, he has been given a reading task which is *too difficult* for him at this particular level of development.

The remedy is a reassessment of (1) the child's level of readiness and (2) the difficulty level of the reading activities the teacher is requiring him to accomplish. Given a fresh start with easier material, the child's self-confidence can be restored before the vicious circle of failure—maladjustment—more failure gets established. We cannot overemphasise the importance of putting a stop to frustrating failure experiences at the earliest possible moment. The child's feeling that 'I am good at reading' is a vital asset in learning to read which should be cultivated with special care, particularly in the earliest stages.

MOTIVATION IN READING READINESS

Another important aspect of the child's psychological development as it effects reading progress is that of motivation, e.g., the child's interest in school activities related to reading and his desire to learn these skills. The studies of Brumbaugh (1940), Stroud (1956) and Burton (1956) all emphasise the importance of motivation in reading success.

Gates (1949) stresses the role of motivation as a factor in causing and correcting difficulties in reading. He describes a study in which a number of children, who had had no experience of learning to read at all, were provided with identical first lessons. Five boxes were used with one of the following words on the top of each box: *ball, bolt, bell, fall, roll.* It was explained to each child that a real ball was in the box whose cover bore that word, and if he correctly picked out this printed word three times in succession he would be allowed to keep the ball. Without exception, the pupils entered upon this game with enthusiasm. Some succceeded at once and gained increasing skill rapidly in similar games with other words; others could not master this task and became very discouraged. There were many types of reaction and many degrees of success, but, as some children's efforts met with repeated failure, their interest began to wane and soon a few pupils showed every evidence of distaste for the task. Gates feels that probably many disabilities in reading might arise in just this way, perhaps from the very first lesson. Clearly, his experiment shows how essential it is to make the tasks to be undertaken and the problems to be solved in learning to read well within the grasp of each individual child's understanding. If the task is too difficult, if the problem is too complex, the child will develop distaste for reading, which is just the reverse of the positive motivation which is needed to make him desire to learn.

Vygotsky's (1962) very important research on beginning reading will be discussed in greater detail in Chapter 5, but we wish to draw attention to one of his main findings now because it related to this problem of motivation. His results led him to conclude that the written form of language must appear a very strange phenomenon to the beginner:

'Writing is also speech without an interlocutor, addressed to an absent or imaginary person or to no one in particular—a situation new and strange to the child. Our studies show that he has little motivation to learn writing when we begin to teach it. He feels no need for it and has only a vague idea of its usefulness.'

Thus there is a general problem of a lack of *intrinsic* motivation to learn to read when children first come to school. True, some children will declare that they 'want to read', but this is usually at best only a sign that some extrinsic motivation to learn to read has been implanted by the child's parents. Very often the child has no real understanding of what 'reading' is. As Reid (1966) found in her research on Scottish young beginners, for them, reading 'is a mysterious activity, to which they come with only the vaguest of expectancies.' The children she studied in their first months at school displayed a 'general lack of any specific expectancies as to what reading was going to be like, of what the activity consisted in, of the purpose and the use of it.'

If the child has such a limited view of its purpose, it is not surprising that Vygotsky concluded that children have little motivation to learn reading and writing. Intrinsic motivation can only begin to develop when the child understands the purpose of the printed or written form of language. He needs to know what it is for. Is it good for something I want to do?

Such motivational readiness is hardly likely to grow on its own. School beginners need to be inducted into the delights of reading and the satisfactions of writing. They need to experience for themselves the fun that can be had from stories in books, the information that can be got from books about something in which one is interested. They need to feel for themselves the rewards of authorship, self-expression and communication of ideas to others.

But this is not simply a problem of *motivation*. To be motivated in this way children must *understand and know* the true purposes of reading and writing. Therefore, we must discuss again in Chapter 5 the problem concerned with developing children's understanding of what exactly reading is. We shall see there that (1) intrinsic motivation and (2) a clear understanding of the way written language is related to spoken language together represent the most important factor of all in reading readiness. In that same chapter we shall describe also some of the practical ways in which teachers and parents can help children to understand and the true purpose and nature of written language and thus develop intrinsic motivation for reading and writing activities. As we shall see later in more detail, the key is sharing with children genuine real-life uses of reading and writing. This is why the most valuable thing parents can do to prepare their children for reading is simply to read books to them. How else can they really *know* that books are worthwhile?

Chapter 5   Intellectual Factors

MENTAL AGE AND INTELLIGENCE

Since the very first experimental investigations into reading readiness, most researchers have emphasised that the level of general mental ability is an extremely important determinant of reading readiness and reading progress. A close relationship between general intelligence and reading would be expected for two important reasons:

1   The ultimate goal of reading is the comprehension of the communication transmitted by the author's writing. This involves, at least, understanding and interpreting the author's ideas.

2   Learning to read requires the development of new concepts of linguistic elements, such as 'word', 'phoneme', 'letter', etc. It also requires reasoning and problem-solving operations in developing the skill of decoding the written form of language back into its primary spoken form.

General intelligence implies all of these abilities; comprehension, interpretation, concept learning, problem-solving, reasoning. Therefore, one would expect intelligence to be closely related to reading readiness, especially if its application to language skills was well developed.

The usual method of studying the importance of general intelligence in learning to read is to obtain intelligence test scores of a group of children soon after entering school and then, at least six months later, to obtain the same children's reading achievement scores. The statistical correlation of the two sets of scores is then calculated. The resulting correlation coefficients in these studies of the relationship between general intelligence and reading achievement have ranged from about ·35 to about ·70, the average being about ·60 which shows a high positive relationship.

The age of the children tested has been found in certain investigations to affect the measure of agreement. Lennon (1950) particularly emphasises the great difference in the correlations between reading ability and intelligence which occur at various grade levels. He found continuously increasing correlations from ·34 for the second grade to ·85 for the eighth grade. This finding was confirmed by Manolakes and Sheldon (1955), and Bond and Tinker (1957).

Most investigators studying the relationship between intelligence and reading at various age levels have proposed what may seem the obvious causal relationship, i.e., that the level of intelligence determines the level of reading ability. Earlier investigators, for example, McLaughlin (1928), Raybold (1929), Deputy (1930), Tinker (1932) and Hayes (1933), have claimed that general mental ability is the most important single factor in determining reading progress. Later investigators, for example, Schonell (1942), Monroe (1932), and Stroud (1956) urge that caution be used when interpreting results. As Schonell (1942) points out:

'This relationship, although high, is by no means absolute. There are not a few intelligent children who fail to make normal progress in reading, and numerous examples of rather dull pupils who read fluently.'

Yet, although such exceptional cases must be admitted, nonetheless it is generally agreed that intelligence is a vital factor in success in learning to read. In more recent studies, both Malmquist (1969) in Sweden, and Vormeland (1967) in Norway have reaffirmed the high correlation between general intelligence and reading ability. Malmquist (1970) concludes that in his research 'the relation was of such an order of magnitude that it definitely confirms the almost unanimous view expressed by previous investigators that intelligence is an important factor in the development of reading ability.'

Teachers must also beware of one of the classic errors of educational research—*the correlation fallacy*. If two measures of behaviour are correlated this is no guarantee that one is the cause of the other. The causal relationship may be in the opposite direction. Or the correlation between the measures may be caused by a third factor not studied. In this particular instance, although high general intelligence seems more likely to be the cause of superior reading attainments, it is unlikely to be such a simple matter. The superior reader reads more and what he learns from books may influence his level of general intelligence. This would explain why the correlation between intelligence and reading attainment was found to increase with age in the three studies mentioned above.

Because intelligence is so closely related to reading ability, it seems reasonable to propose that a certain level of intelligence may be necessary before a child can succeed in learning to read. This conclusion has been the most influential and pervasive one in the literature on reading readiness. The search for the 'teachable moment' in the child's mental development has exercised the minds of many educators. Indeed, the notion that there is some particular mental age which marks the beginning of the stage when children are ready to learn to read, has been the 'philosopher's stone' of the psychology of learning to read.

According to Betts (1946) the most widely quoted and misquoted study on the minimal mental age necessary for readiness for learning to read is that of Morphett and Washburne. In the early 1930s these two authors made two investigations of this problem at Winnetka; the first, in 1928, involved 141 children for one semester; the second, made the following year, involved 100 children for one year. For the first study, the *Detroit First Grade Intelligence Test* was used to appraise mental ability, and reading progress was measured by the number of steps each pupil had completed by February in the *Winnetka Primary Reading Materials.* Each step represented a reader in the series, and the eight first-grade teachers concerned agreed that children who were ready to read on entering in September usually completed thirteen steps by the following February. An additional check was made by the use of a sight-word test; on this test, the teachers concerned felt that the recognition of thirty-seven words in February would indicate satisfactory progress. Hence thirteen steps and thirty-seven sight words were accepted as the measure of the minimum degree of satisfactory progress.

For the second study, the *Detroit* and *Pintner-Cunningham* tests were used to determine mental ages, and the *Gray Standardised Oral Reading Check Test* and the sight-word list were used to measure reading progress. In their data, Morphett and Washburne grouped the children according to their mental ages, and calculated the percentages in each group making satisfactory progress in reading. Both experiments showed that very little, if any, progress was made by the children with mental ages below six years, but that the increase in percentage of successes rose sharply at the mental age of six and a half years. Morphett and Washburne conclude:

'Consequently it seems safe to state that, by postponing the teaching of reading until children reach a mental level of six and a half years, teachers can generally decrease the chances of failure and discouragement and can correspondingly increase their efficiency.'

The details of this study have been included because as Downing (1966) points out:

'Although the generalised finding of this research of Morphett and Washburne is often quoted in elementary education texts, the details of the method and sample used appear to have been forgotten. From the details given it can be seen that the sample was small, eight teachers were involved and the measure of the minimum degree of satisfactory progress quite arbitrary and related specifically to the *Winnetka Primary Reading Materials*. It is obvious that generalisation from this limited study to the world-wide reading situation was quite unjustified, yet this is what happened.'

In similar experiments and studies, Bigelow (1934), Witty and Kopel (1936a, b and c), Dolch and Bloomster (1937) and Dean (1939) all claimed to have found that a minimum mental age was required for successful reading, and mental ages of six, six and a half and seven were mentioned in these studies. A careful study of these investigations makes it clear that the minimum mental age found necessary for successful reading depended entirely on the criteria of successful reading, i.e., what the researchers considered to be 'reading'.

In other words, the most that could be claimed for any one of these studies is that they had discovered the minimal mental age required to handle the task of learning *by that particular method of teaching and with those particular books and teaching materials*. Each author made the error of over generalising his results from readiness to read the particular materials used in his experiment to readiness to read anything. In the years following this phase of research on reading readiness, the generalisation that children were incapable of learning to read before reaching a mental age of six or six and a half years was widely accepted. In America many writers, too numerous to mention, stated categorically that there is a minimum mental age necessary for success in first-grade reading, and many school systems in America accepted these statements and put the underlying ideas into practice. For example, Betts (1946) reported that in Los Angeles one of the guides to teachers in determining the point at which reading may begin with promise of success was 'a mental age of 76–80 months'. Dolch (1950) has indicated that in some school systems the postponing of beginning reading is sometimes done by keeping children in kindergarten until they have reached a mental age of six and a half. These notions even spread to other countries with different languages, although no one knew whether the problem of learning to read in them was more or less difficult than learning to read in the English language. 'Reading' was assumed to be the same in every language.

In recent years, however, other investigators have criticised the concept of a minimum mental age for reading for all children in all circumstances, and growing evidence is being provided to show that children can, in suitable circumstances, learn to read successfully with a mental age well below six years six months. The obvious example of this is in the British schools where children conventionally start compulsory schooling at five years and are fairly quickly introduced to reading. Most British children are actually reading quite successfully before they attain a mental age of six years six months. Lynn has stated that:

'The notion of reading readiness at the mental age of six to eight years is almost universally accepted in the United States and very widely in Britain by 75 per cent of head teachers according to Morris (1959).'

With regard to British educational thought on this question, Lynn is misleading in asserting that a minimum mental age of six to eight is accepted 'very widely' in Britain. Yates (1954) has noted that:

'There is considerable opposition in this country (Britain) to the idea that positive steps should be taken to ascertain that children have reached the stage in their development at which formal instruction in reading should begin.'

Again Morris (1959), and Thackray (1965, 1971) found that it was only the exceptional child who had not started a reader by the end of the third term in school, and most had started formal reading by the end of the second term. This means most children would have started reading with chronological and mental ages below six years. In the classroom situation, Morris (1959) has suggested that teachers are guided more by 'instinct' than by mental age. The teacher's 'instinct' usually means her observation of each child's desire to learn to read by his showing an interest in books, and the teacher's noting of the child's ability to recognise and remember words.

In Thackray's (1965) investigation with British children, it was found that a minimum mental age of five and a half years was necessary for the beginning of formal reading and for making a satisfactory progress in learning to read under the typical circumstances of British schools.

Regarding the growing evidence of children learning to read successfully with mental ages of below six and a half years, the studies of Dolbear (1912), Terman (1918), Terman and Oden (1947), Diack (1960), Lynn (1963), Fowler (1962) and Thackray (1971) provide evidence of very young children under the age of three learning to read. However, a careful study of the cases described suggests that the children involved were above-average intellectually, instruction was individual and enjoyable, and, perhaps more important, by 'reading' was really meant the recognition of letters or of words. Fowler, Lynn, and Thackray all reported that their daughters quickly lost interest in the 'reading' activity, which suggests the reading was mechanical, the effort was unrewarding, and the activity was not very meaningful. This kind of reading is with the eyes and the voice, but not with the understanding which comes from experience and the development of concepts.

Durkin (1959, 1961, 1963 and 1964) has made a number of studies which show that children can learn to read at home, with mental ages of three, four and five. From the data provided we learn that these early readers tended to be children who were persistent, perfectionist, eager to keep up with older siblings, and curious. Again the evidence suggests that the children were precocious, instruction was individual given by parents or older siblings and by 'reading', word recognition only was implied. However, some of Durkin's early readers were only of normal intelligence, and her later follow-up studies show that an early start seems to be most helpful to those children who were at this lower level of intelligence.

In a critical appraisal of the minimum age concept, those studies which investigated children of average ability in normal or near normal classroom situations have most relevance. As Holmes (1962) has pointed out:

'Other things being equal the earliest age at which a child can be taught to read is a function of the amount of time or help the teacher can give the pupil.'

The amount of time a busy class teacher can devote to each child is very limited, and of course most children do not learn to read until they start school.

Davidson's (1931) experiment is a little nearer the classroom situation as she used groups of *five* children, though they were pre-school children. She conducted her experiment with a bright three-year-old group, a normal four-year-old group and a dull five-year-old group—all having Stanford-Binet mental ages of approximately four years. Each group received ten-minute reading lessons daily for four months, and reading tests were given at the end of that period. After four months the bright three-year-old children recognised on average 129·4 words out of context, the average four-year-olds 55·3 words, and the dull five-year-olds 40 words. This experiment is often quoted to support the claim that children can learn to read with mental ages of four, but it must be noted that when the children's retention was tested, four months after the close of the experiment, the dull children recognised on average only nine words; this raises another question as to whether the effort to teach five-year-old children with a mental age of four was economical.

Probably the most outstanding contribution to the question under discussion was that of Gates (1937), who examined studies made of four groups of children in ordinary classroom situations. In the first of the four groups where modern and effective instruction well-adjusted to individual differences was provided, a mental age of five years appeared to be sufficient for learning to read; in a second group conditions were less favourable and a mental age of five and a half was necessary; in a third group the teaching conditions were still more inferior and a mental age of six years was required to make satisfactory progress; in a fourth group representing the opposite extreme from the first group, children with a mental age of six and a half fared none too well, and some with mental ages of seven or above had difficulty. Gates showed that in the normal classroom situation children could learn to read with mental ages below six years, but he did note that practically all near failures fell into the group with a mental age of less than five years. His main finding was that:

'Statements concerning the necessary mental age at which a pupil can be instructed to learn to read are essentially meaningless. The age for learning to read under one program, or with the methods employed by one teacher, may be entirely different from that required under other circumstances.'

Thus, the evidence from the research discussed in this chapter indicates that children have been taught to read, somewhat mechanically, with mental ages of four or less, but the children tended to be (though not always) above average in intelligence, and they were taught individually or in very small groups. In the normal classroom situation, the mental age requirements will vary with the methods and materials used, but it would seem that a mental age of at least five or five and a half years is necessary for success in any of the traditional methods of teaching reading in the English language, as there is evidence both in America and Britain to show that worthwhile progress in reading is not made where mental ages fall below five years.

However, even though it is possible with appropriate methods and materials to teach children to read with a mental age of five years, the question remains as to whether it is desirable to do so. Is the time and effort expended in teaching an average five-year-old to read justified by the progress he makes, bearing in mind that the stage of reading readiness is only reached when the child can learn to read *both easily and profitably*? Some experimenters in recent years have deliberately set out to make reading more easy and more profitable for younger children. We may consider this question further when we review these experiments in Chapter 6.

PERCEPTUAL ABILITIES OF VISUAL AND AUDITORY DISCRIMINATION

The structure of general intelligence is a complex problem. According to Harris (1961) some abilities, such as remembering and attending, are hard to distinguish from general intelligence in young children but other abilities, such as the perceptual abilities of visual and auditory discrimination do seem to be relatively specific. Vernon's (1961) specialist work on the structure of human abilities, however, would suggest that 'g' (the general factor in intelligence) and the major group factor, 'V:ed' (verbal-numerical-educational factor), are of greatest importance in determining differences in reading ability. One would expect, therefore, that tests of auditory and visual discrimination would have slightly higher correlations with reading attainments, simply because they test the application of intelligence in activities which are especially significant for the task of learning to read.

Two important parts of the skill of reading are, firstly, discriminating the visual stimuli of printed letters and words, and, secondly, of associating such visual stimuli with the auditory elements of the spoken language. Hence, one would anticipate the abilities of visual and auditory discrimination to be closely related to reading readiness and to reading progress, and research shows that this is indeed the case.

Durrell (1956) states that the minimum requirement in the visual discrimination of word elements appears to be the ability to match letters. He says:

'If the child cannot tell letters apart it is futile for the teacher to teach him words. He cannot attach meaning and name to a word that he cannot recognise when he sees it, a few seconds later.'

The 'phoneme' is the basic unit of sound with which we are concerned in auditory discrimination as related to learning to read. By 'phonemes', we mean those sounds of a language which represent changes in meaning. For example, the change in vowel sound in *hat* and *hut* is phonemic because it results in a change in meaning. Of the auditory perception of phonemes, which is somewhat harder to observe and measure, Durrell, in the same book, says:

'It consists in being able to notice the separate sounds in spoken words—in the ability to identify the M-M-M sound in mother, magic and machine. Unless the child notices the separate sounds in spoken words there is no sense for him in the way words are spelled. While he may acquire a small sight vocabulary without this ability, he quickly runs into confusion with words which look very much alike. He has no system that will relieve this confusion.'

Typical of the earlier experiments designed to investigate the relationship between visual perception and reading success were those of Sister Mary of the Visitation (1929), Fendrick (1935), and Gates, Bond and Russell (1939). The correlation coefficients in these investigations were between ·5 and ·6 when verbal material was used, but where non-verbal visual perception tests were used, lower correlation coefficients were found. More recent investigations carried out by Sister Mary Nila (1940), Durrell, Murphy and Junkins (1941), Harrington and Durrell (1955) and Nicholson (1958) have shown quite clearly that visual and auditory discrimination are more important than mental age in reading readiness and reading success. Sister Mary Nila's experiment is typical of these investigations.

She tested 300 first grade entrants in eleven classes in nine schools, during their first few weeks in school (September). Four individual and four group tests were given of various readiness skills; in the following January and July the same children were given reading achievement tests and correlations made. Sister Mary Nila found that, of all the tests, the four factors that had the greatest relationship to reading achievement were, in order of importance, auditory discrimination ability, visual discrimination ability, range of information and mental age.

In his first experimental investigation into the reading readiness of British children, Thackray (1965) tested a representative sample of 182 children for reading readiness skills when commencing their second term in school (average age 5 years 4 months), and also for the other important factors in reading readiness; general intelligence, home environment, and emotional and personal attitudes. The following measures were used:

1 *The Harrison-Stroud Reading Readiness Profiles* (adapted for British use) consisting of tests of using symbols, making visual discriminations, using the context, making auditory discriminations, and using context and auditory clues.

2 *The Kelvin Measurement of Ability Test for Infants* (Fleming), and teachers' ratings of general ability.

3 A multiple choice picture vocabulary profile, constructed by the investigator, and teachers' ratings of language and speech.

4 Teachers' ratings of self-confidence, cooperation with adults, cooperation with other children, persistence, stability and prevailing attitude.

Later, when commencing their fourth and fifth terms in school, the average ages being 6 years, and 6 years 4 months respectively, the same children were given parallel forms of the *Southgate Group Reading Test 1* (Southgate, 1959). The raw scores obtained from all these measures were standardised and the earlier results were correlated with the later results by the product moment method.

In the sample selected, the reading readiness tests proved a valid measure of readiness for reading (·59), and, of these, auditory and visual discrimination correlated the most highly with reading achievement (·53 and ·50 respectively); general ability was found to be important (·47) but not so important as auditory and visual discrimination; home environment was found to be of lesser importance (·42), and emotional and personal attitudes relatively unimportant (·10–·36). It is interesting to note that these results are very similar to those found in the more recent of the American experiments, although the British children were, on average, a year younger than their American counterparts. They also add to the growing evidence that (as would be expected) visual and auditory discrimination are more important in the early stages of learning to read than general mental ability.

In Thackray's (1971) second investigation the aim was to ascertain experimentally the difference between the reading readiness requirements necessary for satisfactory reading progress of children learning to read with i.t.a. (Initial Teaching Alphabet), and children learning to read with t.o. (traditional orthography—the conventional English alphabet and spelling). This investigation was conducted on similar lines to the first one. After six weeks in school two matched groups of i.t.a. and t.o. children (approximately 150 in each group) were given tests of visual and auditory discrimination, mental ability and vocabulary. In the children's third, fourth, sixth and ninth terms in school, reading achievement tests were administered, transliterated i.t.a. versions of the t.o. tests being used initially with the i.t.a. group. One of the statistical procedures was to correlate the earlier results on the reading readiness measures with the later results on the reading achievement tests, and the following averaged correlation coefficients for 238 children were established towards the end of the children's second and third years in school when the reading achievement tests were given in t.o. to both the i.t.a. and the t.o. groups:

	End of second year	End of third year
Visual discrimination	·48	·58
Auditory discrimination	·46	·41
General ability	·38	·38
Vocabulary development	·38	·44

The above coefficients of correlation show again that visual and auditory discrimination have a substantial relationship with reading progress which is even greater than general mental ability either in learning to read t.o. through the medium of i.t.a., or in learning to read with t.o. through the medium of t.o. from the beginning.

As further evidence of the importance of visual discrimination in learning to read Nicholson (1958), Olson (1958) and Gavel (1958) have all shown in their experiments carried out in America that of all tests of readiness those which measure knowledge of the names of letters provide the best prediction of success in learning to read. In order to name a letter correctly, a child must be able to discriminate visually that letter shape from a different one, and so the results are hardly surprising. But the teacher should beware of naïve extensions that have been made to this conclusion. This finding does *not* necessarily prove that *teaching* children letter-names will help them in learning to read. (Indeed, as we shall see in Chapter 6 there is definite evidence that it does *not* help.)

What these various researches do show is that the importance of intelligence increases when it is related more directly to behaviour of specific significance in reading, i.e., in this instance, visual and auditory discrimination.

In the older conventional view of reading readiness it was generally believed that these perceptual abilities in visual and auditory discrimination depended on maturation which could not be hurried by teaching. Furthermore, it was thought that the level of such perceptual abilities necessary for reading readiness was not normally reached until about the age of six or seven.

However, more recently Downing (1963) and Lynn (1963) have suggested that the perceptual abilities required by children for successful reading have been overestimated and that the theory of maturation which has been described by Benda (1954) as 'a biological process which cannot be accelerated by artificial means' is no longer tenable. Benda's maturational theory was based on a number of studies of children's abilites in copying letters or figures. These studies suggested to Benda that children with mental ages below six could not perceive words or letters, and in this context it has been found that a mental age of seven is required before a child can copy a diamond accurately in the Stanford-Binet test. Lynn's comment on this finding is that:

'All this evidence shows is that children do not *draw* accurately until this mental age . . . However, . . . when naming or pointing is used instead of drawing as an index of perceptual ability, it is evident that children can make perceptual differentiation at considerably lower mental ages.'

Lynn's view is supported by evidence from the studies of Dolbear (1912), Terman (1918), Diack (1960) and Fowler (1962) which show that children with mental ages of less than five can perceive enough detail in words to help them to recognise them. Thackray (1965, 1971) showed in his investigation that British children, soon after entering school at the age of five, could tackle simple tests of visual and auditory discrimination very confidently and score very satisfactorily, when a simple pencil mark on the paper was all that was required in answering them.

The maturational approach of Benda (1954), Hymes (1958) and Olson (1959) posits that parents and teachers cannot accelerate the child's development of readiness; on the other hand, Peterson (1937), Scott (1947), Sister Nila (1953) and Bradley (1955), among others, have shown that teaching programmes designed to help children get ready for reading have developed readiness and Teegarden (1932), Hildreth (1950), Durrell and Murphy (1953) and Lineham (1958) have shown that specific training in visual and auditory discrimination brings about improvement in these abilities.

The weight of evidence, therefore, seems to favour the view that the perceptual abilities of children should not be underestimated, and more consideration must be given to the extent to which we can develop these various abilities through training. More about this will be said in Chapter 6, pages 73 to 79.

CONCEPTUAL DEVELOPMENT AND SPECIFIC
REASONING ABILITIES

Just as intelligence becomes an even more powerful factor when related to perceptual abilities used in reading, so also one would predict that the development of concepts and reasoning abilities which are specific to the tasks of learning to read and write would be not only heavily loaded with the factor of general intelligence, but also, because of their specific relevance, they would be even more highly correlated with achievements in reading than mental age alone.

There are no correlational studies on this question, but in recent years a fair amount of evidence has been discovered that these cognitive factors in conceptual development and reasoning abilities may be the most important of all of the foundations of readiness for learning to read. The research evidence comes from two areas of investigation: (i) the study of the causes of reading disability, and (ii) studies of young children's cognitive development.

1 *Cognitive confusion in reading disability*
M. D. Vernon's (1957) book, *Backwardness in Reading*, is a report of the most thorough and rigorously scientific review of research on reading disability ever conducted in Britain or America. Professor Vernon found that reading disability has many possible causes, yet there is one symptom that crops up over and over again in descriptions of children who have failed to learn to read. Therefore, she concludes:

'Thus the fundamental and basic characteristic of reading disability appears to be cognitive confusion and lack of system.'

Vernon defines cognitive confusion as follows:

'The child with real reading disability . . . may indeed have learnt that printed words have some relation to spoken words; and, with a few simple words, he has memorised the spoken word that corresponds to a particular shape. But he does not seem to understand why: it might be quite an arbitrary association. He appears hopelessly uncertain and confused as to why certain successions of printed letters should correspond to certain phonetic sounds in words . . . To make this association demands a particular type of reasoning process.'

In case of reading disability, 'the fundamental trouble appears to be a failure in development of this reasoning process.' Also, 'the backward reader remains in a state of confusion over the whole process.'

Intelligence is often defined in terms of reasoning ability. Hence the rather high correlation between general intelligence and reading attainments is not surprising. But what Vernon's conclusion indicates even more strongly is that reading involves '*a particular type* of reasoning process', which must be of much greater importance in learning to read than the *general* reasoning ability tested on conventional intelligence tests. When this specific reasoning process fails to develop adequately, the symptom, according to Vernon, is that the disabled reader 'remains in a state of confusion over the whole process'. Vernon's use of the word 'remains' in this quotation is significant. It suggests that the normal development of this 'particular type of reasoning process' is a process of clearing up an initial cognitive confusion about the reading process and replacing it by an increasing *cognitive clarity*. In the following pages we shall see that this development of an appropriate logic for learning to read does appear to be a key factor in the progress of normal beginners.

2 *The development of cognitive clarity*

Piaget's (1959) research on the development of children's language and its relation to their thinking processes provides many insights for the teacher who seeks to understand the logic of the child when he is at the age when most children are first introduced to the tasks of learning to read and write. The remarkable difference between the logic of the five- or six-year-old as compared with that of older individuals is of special importance for understanding the problems of learning the written form of language. It would be a grave error to assume that the young child's perception of the processes of reading and writing is the same as that of the adult who desires to teach him these useful skills.

Although Piaget himself has not applied his theories to the problem of children's cognitive development as specifically related to learning literacy, another scholar did attempt to do so. Vygotsky (1962) was deeply interested in Piaget's work and replicated and extended some of it. Of special interest is Vygotsky's investigation of the problem of 'the tremendous lag between the school child's oral and written language.' His research led him to conclude:

1 'Our studies show that it is the abstract quality of written language that is the main stumbling block.'

2 'He (the child) has little motivation to learn writing when we begin to teach it. He feels no need for it and has only a vague idea of its usefulness.' (Also quoted earlier in our chapter on motivation.)

He points out the essential difference between cognitive functioning in written as compared with spoken language:

'Written language demands conscious work because its relationship to inner speech is different from that of oral speech: the latter precedes inner speech in the course of development, while written speech follows inner speech and presupposes its existence (the act of writing implying a translation from inner speech).'

In summary, we would predict from Piaget's theory that there would be important differences between the young child's view of language and the way it is perceived by adults. Vygotsky's research confirms this. The child does not see the expressive and communicative purposes of written language. As Piaget showed, he is not very concerned about communication of any kind at this egocentric stage of development. Written language, because it is one step further removed from immediate concrete reality, is of even less interest as a means of communication than speaking. Piaget's theory would also lead us to anticipate that the abstract concepts and principles involved in relating written language to speech would be difficult for young children to understand because of their primitive level of cognitive development. Again, Vygotsky's research confirms this hypothesis. It is this *abstract* nature of the task which makes it hard to learn the written form of language at this stage.

Independent confirmation of the importance of specific cognitive development is provided by the results of Reid's (1966) intensive studies of twelve five-year-olds in their first year at a primary school in Scotland. She interviewed these girls and boys in a free conversational manner three times; two months, five months and nine months after their first entry to school. As we mentioned previously in our chapter on motivation, she discovered that for such young beginners reading is 'a mysterious activity, to which they come with only the vaguest of expectancies.' They displayed, she says, a 'general lack of any specific expectancies of what reading was going to be like, of what the activity consisted in, of the purpose and the use of it.' Another of Reid's chief findings was that these children had great difficulty in understanding such abstract technical terms as 'word', 'letter', 'sound', etc. As the year progressed, Reid found that the children became clearer about the task they were trying to learn, and their use of technical linguistic terms became more consistent.

Downing (1970a and b, 1971) replicated Reid's interview study with twelve children in the south of England. His results confirmed her findings, but Downing extended Reid's method to include other tests and experiments in order to throw further light on the developmental process which lies behind these children's increasing ability to use linguistic concepts in solving problems in learning to read. Downing's results provide the link between Vernon's study of backwardness in reading and Reid's and Vygotsky's research on children's thinking about reading.

The 'cognitive confusion', which Vernon found to be the chief symptom of reading retardation in older pupils, was found by Downing to be the normal state of the young beginner in the primary school. A minority of Downing's five-year-olds remained in a state of cognitive confusion at the end of the year. The others made varying degrees of progress towards cognitive clarity about the task of learning to read. These children's responses, as the year moved on, could be compared with the clearing of fog. Gradually out of confusion came a clearer and clearer understanding of the nature of the learning and problem-solving tasks they were required to undertake. This cognitive clarification was particularly notable in five characteristics of their development. The more progress they made towards general cognitive clarity:

1 The better these children understood the communication purpose of the written form of language.

2 The clearer was their conception of the function of symbols.

3 The nearer their concepts of linguistic segments, such as 'word' and 'sound' approached those of the teacher.

4 The better was their corresponding spontaneous command of the abstract technical terminology of language.

5 The better they understood the process of decoding alphabetic letters to speech sounds and *vice versa* in encoding.

Cognitive factors are emphasised also by the leading authority on reading readiness in the German language. In her article 'The concept of reading readiness in Austria' Schenk-Danzinger (1967) bases her judgement of the appropriate age for beginning reading on the child's development of *abstract thinking* abilities. This, she points out, must depend to an important extent on the level of abstract thinking required in learning to read in different languages. She concludes that for alphabetic languages the essential intellectual ability to analyse a word into its abstract parts, the separate phonemes, does not usually develop adequately before the age of 6–7 years. This view accords well with Downing's theory of the importance of developing cognitive clarity in the process of learning to read.

Further support for this theory comes from a recent investigation of reading readiness in Norway. Gjessing (1967) found that among twenty tests included in a factor analysis, only one factor was associated with 'rapid achievement of exceptionally good reading ability'. He identifies this factor as representing 'functions such as reasoning and comprehension of symbols'.

Taken together, the studies of Piaget, Vygotsky, Vernon, Reid, Schenk-Danzinger, Gjessing and Downing provide evidence that a very important factor in reading readiness is the child's development of concepts and reasoning abilities which are specific (a) to the skills of reading and writing and (b) to the tasks involved in learning them.

Thus, we conclude that intellectual development contains the

65

key factors in reading readiness. General intelligence is an important factor, but of even greater significance are those three factors which are specifically related to learning to read:

1 Visual discrimination
2 Auditory discrimination
3 The cognitive development of the special concepts and reasoning abilities which are used in learning to read.

As we shall see in Chapter 6, these key factors are all amenable to modification by the teacher, either through special training for the child or through simplification of the learning tasks presented to children in their first experiences in reading.

Chapter 6 Readiness Training

CAN READING READINESS BE CULTIVATED EARLIER?

The validity of the conventional concept of reading readiness currently is under fire, both in America and in Britain. For example, in America, McCracken (1952) and Flesch (1955) feel the idea of reading readiness should be abandoned, and in Britain Lynn writes:

'. . . it seems doubtful whether the concept of reading readiness has sufficient substance to be worth retaining.'

As Thackray (1971) points out, the validity of the conventional concept of readiness has been questioned in the light of three educational developments of recent years:
1 The growing evidence of children learning to read with mental ages of well below six years, which used to be the fairly widely accepted minimum mental age limit for successful reading. This evidence has been described in Chapter 5, page 57.
2 A closer scrutiny of the perceptual abilities required by children for successful reading. This evidence has been described in Chapter 5, pages 57–61.
3 The introduction of newer methods of teaching reading which may simplify the tasks involved in what we call 'reading'. These methods will be discussed on pages 82–8.
Certainly, the evidence runs strongly counter to the conventional view of reading readiness, but, if these traditional educational beliefs are to be scrapped, how shall we replace them? There are two groups of opinions on this controversy. Some would abolish the idea of readiness altogether. Others would retain it but bring it up-to-date and into line with modern research findings on children and the language they have to learn to read. In this chapter first we will discuss the view that the concept of reading readiness should be abolished altogether. The other view-point will also be presented together with outlines of the methods which have been proposed for helping children to get ready to read sooner than they would if just left to nature.
Impatience with the whole notion of reading readiness has always been a feature of the outlook of a small group of educators. While the majority of American reading experts were

in favour of postponing systematic reading instruction until the child showed signs of readiness, yet there was always a minority view which favoured starting all children in reading from the beginning of the first grade: this latter approach was termed 'forcing' by Olson and Hughes (1944).

Curiously, this impatience with the concept of reading readiness has often been associated with a demand for phonic methods of teaching from the very beginning. For example, Flesch (1955) and Durrell (1956) in America, and Daniels and Diack (1956) and Gattegno (1962) in Britain feel that intensive phonic instruction should play an important part in the very early stages of reading. The tendency of these methods using systematic phonic instruction is to ignore the readiness period and to begin formal reading very soon after the children enter school. For example, Flesch condemns readiness programmes as a waste of time, and Gattegno who has designed the *Words in Colour* system with its highly phonic teaching methods, believes that we underestimate children, and his approach makes no concessions to a readiness period of creative activities.

To combine phonic teaching methods with the dismissal of the whole idea of reading readiness is very curious, because it is just such abstract phonetic concepts involved in those phonic methods which young children have most difficulty in understanding, as the researches of Piaget, Vygotsky, Reid and Downing, referred to earlier in Chapter 5, indicate so clearly.

Also it is just this type of phonic learning which the Austrian authority on readiness, Schenk-Danzinger, singles out as being too difficult for most children to understand before the age of six years. She states:

'In preschool age the child already possesses all prerequisitions for reading in word-signs (i.e. whole words). Maturity for assigning sound-meanings to letter-signs, however, does not develop before the age of 6–7.'

This, Schenk-Danzinger indicates, is because, 'Easy as the alphabetic system may seem, its acquisition requires a higher degree of abstract thinking than is necessary for the reading of logograms.'

In another report of his research, Downing (1970b) points out that the young child's natural difficulty in handling abstract concepts is fundamentally related to his other initial problem, i.e., that he does not readily see the true purpose of the written form of language. He suggests, therefore, that:

'naïve formal methods of instruction in the meaning of abstract technical terms such as "word" or "sound" produce worse than the child's mental 'vacuum" envisaged by Vygotsky. Their more unfortunate consequence is their failure to provide correct orientation towards the true purpose of written language in human expression and communication. This can be given only by genuine experiences of written language which fulfil such purposes for the young beginner.'

Such experiences are hardly likely to be provided by methods of teaching which emphasize the analysis of language into its abstract elements, as is usually done in most phonic methods.

Recently, one of the authors of this book met an 'exception which proves the rule'. He was visiting a first-grade classroom on an Indian reservation in Canada. It was during the last week of the school year. One bright six-year-old girl read and wrote with quite a lot of help from phonic analysis. In discussing her good progress with the teacher, this author noted her interesting comment that this girl was the only one in the class who was 'thinking phonetically'.

It is this sign of cognitive clarity which is noticeably absent in most young beginners, and 'forcing' methods at best can do little more than gloss over the cognitive confusion which is bound to exist until appropriate experiences bring about real clarification.

In recent years there has been a trend to introduce reading at even younger ages than usual in America. Many school districts have begun to teach reading at the kindergarten stage instead of waiting until first grade. One example of a report on such a project is that published by Kelley (1965). She describes, first of all, a pilot study and then tells about a more rigorously controlled experiment which followed it. It is illuminating to compare the methods of the pilot study with those of the scientific experiment and note the difference in their results, which was produced quite unintentionally.

Of the pilot programme, Kelley writes, 'No child reads who doesn't want to, no child is kept out who wants to be in the reading group.' This sounds familiar to British teachers who have worked with children of the same age level (5 to 6 years) using the same kind of approach. The preliminary evaluation of the pilot programme showed that the children who had learned to read in kindergarten were, by second grade, not only significantly advanced in reading skills, but also more positive in their attitudes to reading.

These results encouraged the undertaking of a more rigorously controlled experiment for the purposes of the scientific design of the research. Kelley reports that the experimenters 'frustrated some bright children in the control group who wished to read and some others in the experimental group who did not wish to read. While it was nearly possible to keep the lid on the control group, it was virtually impossible to teach some children in the experimental group to read.' What is particularly interesting is Kelley's report of the children's attitudes measured on a self-reporting inventory at the end of the kindergarten year, 'It was found that the control group had more favourable attitudes towards school.' This finding is buried amongst a great deal of other data and it is not specially emphasized by Kelley, who seemed to regard the whole experiment in introducing reading into the kindergarten as a great success. But what Kelley's study brings out, quite accidentally, is the danger of assuming that 'reading' (whatever that may mean in this situation) can be pushed down from the first grade into kindergarten—without the kind of modifications which Kelley mentions were used intuitively in the original pilot study, but not in the more rigorous (and rigid) scientific experiment.

Kelley's report serves also to show the real value of the concept of reading readiness. Mass teaching of reading to all children at age five or even at age six ignores important individual differences in children's abilities and styles of learning. Even if conventional notions of reading readiness are untenable in the light of recent educational research and development, one must recognise that the older view of readiness did encourage teachers to pace the introduction and teaching of reading to the needs of the individual. Complete abolition of the concept of reading readiness could be a retrograde step if it led to pressuring unwilling children into reading. Therefore, our conclusion is that the reading readiness concept should be retained, but modified to take account of modern developments in this field.

READINESS TRAINING

The other group of writers who believe a new view of reading readiness is needed, does not wish to see the concept abolished altogether. They seek only to move further away from the conventional view that readiness must wait for natural maturation.

This is by no means a new idea either. For example, the *Twenty-fourth Year Book of the National Society for the Study of Education,* published in 1925 in America, recommended that reading instruction should be preceded by *pre-reading activities,* and since that time many writers such as Gates (1949), Stroud (1956) and Bond and Tinker (1957), have cautioned against starting formal reading too early, before the child is ready and without such pre-reading experiences. They point out quite forcibly the harm that can be done if such a thing happens. For example Stroud writes:

'A pretty good defence could be made for the thesis that our reading clinics and remedial reading programs are testimony to the unwisdom of our haste.'

Many writers who advocate delaying the start of formal reading where necessary, emphasise the fact that the time before reading commences should be used to prepare the child by a broad reading readiness programme. Investigations into the value of reading readiness programmes are generally favourable and have shown that delaying more formal systematic instruction in reading for a few weeks or months and replacing it with reading readiness activities certainly, at the very least, does not retard progress later. Among the more important experiments of this nature are those of Peterson (1937), Scott (1947), Sister Nila (1953) and Bradley (1955) in America and Gardner (1948) in Britain.

For example, Bradley matched two groups of first-grade children, each group consisting of 31 children on the basis of sex, chronological age, I.Q. and the father's socio-economic status. The experimental group participated in a programme which was built on the concept of readiness, and designed to stimulate growth in all aspects. Formal systematic instruction in reading was not given to any child in the experimental group until he was considered ready. In the control group, in contrast, such formal instruction was provided immediately on entrance to grade I. After two years, test results clearly indicated that the experimental group children who had participated in the readiness programme attained a degree of achievement in reading equal to the control group. By the end of the third year the experimental group was up to the normal standard in reading and equalled the progress of the control group; also, by the end of the same year the experimental group was above standard in other skills, such as work-study skills and basic language skills, and showed slight gains, some statistically significant, over the control group.

All these experiments indicate the value of finding out the individual differences and needs of the children when they enter school and of substituting a reading readiness programme where children are not ready to commence formal reading.

But, even if we assume that this individualisation of the teaching will be our first rule in deciding how to treat each child according to his own level of readiness, there remains *the practical problem for the teacher—what exactly shall I do to increase each child's level of readiness for the more formal tasks of learning to read and write?*

Very many different reading readiness programmes have

been proposed. Before we study some typical examples, we should try to put the whole field into perspective by categorising these different approaches according to their aims. To do this, we will adopt an idea from a different area of psychology. Rodger, when Professor of Occupational Psychology in the University of London, some years ago proposed that there seemed to be two ways of going about improving people's productivity at work; one can either fit the man for the job, or fit the job to the man. These are complementary ways of approaching this problem and should normally be tackled together. In a way, Professor Rodger is talking about our problem, too. His concern is for a man's readiness for work. In industry, for example, on the one hand, one can select an individual who is already well-fitted (i.e. 'ready') for the job or one can train him (i.e. give him 'job-readiness activities'). On the other hand, the job could be changed. One can modify the machines or methods used in industry to fit them better to the 'job-readiness' of the men who will use them.

In other words, 'readiness' implies some kind of gap between the psychological state of the human being and the task he must accomplish. *'Readiness activities', whether in industry or in education are a means of narrowing the gap between the state of the human individual and the conditions of the task to be mastered.* The gap can be narrowed either by changing the individual or by changing the task, or, of course, by doing both these things.

If we look at the various attempts to facilitate the early learning of reading we shall see that they can be classified according to whether they try *either to fit the child for reading or to fit reading to the child.*

FITTING THE CHILD FOR READING

As in industry, so in education there are two ways of fitting the individual to the task. One is by selection, the other by training.

By 'selection', we can pick out the children who are ready to begin formal reading and we can select children who are ready for different levels of a readiness programme. This may be done by objective testing or by teachers' subjective judgments. These methods of appraising readiness will be discussed in Chapter 7. Here, we will only indicate how very important we consider this appraisal and selection to be. At the present time, particularly in America, where there is so much demand that children should begin reading earlier, this need to check each pupil's individual abilities and styles of learning is more important than ever. In another recent article, 'Should today's children start reading earlier?' Downing (1968a) concluded that while *some* children should begin earlier than they are being allowed to in many American schools, they should do so only if certain conditions were met:

'Above all, *if* great care is taken to cater for individual differences in the capacities and experiences of the children, the younger the pupils, the greater the need for an individual approach.'

By 'training', we can provide a range of activities and experiences which will help children to develop the basic understandings and sub-skills needed for learning to read and write. There are many such programmes which are designed to give 'training' in readiness (although the term 'training' is not usually appropriate at this level in education because it smacks too much of formal instructional methods).

Most of the commercially published methods of changing the child to fit him better for the task of reading consist in batteries of perceptual training activities planned to improve children's visual and auditory discrimination abilities. Other aspects of readiness are not usually covered in commercial materials, although they may be included in more informal reading readiness programmes devised by teachers.

How effective are such attempts to train children's readiness for reading? This is the question investigated in a recent study by Ollila (1970). First, he examined the feasibility of training at all. How far is it possible to improve either visual or auditory discrimination through training young children. He reviewed the visual discrimination training experiments reported in 17 original researches*, and concluded that 'to a certain extent skill in visual discrimination can be improved by direct training at the kindergarten level.' Another recently published report of an experiment in visual perception training reached the same conclusion (Faustman, 1968).

Far fewer studies have investigated the trainability of auditory discrimination. Ollila's review of those conducted by McNeil and Keisler (1963), McNeil and Stone (1965) and Silvaroli and Wheelock (1966) led him to conclude that 'kindergarten children including those from low socio-economic status levels do benefit from some sort of auditory discrimination training.'

*Davis *et al.* (1949), Cantor (1955), Schaeffer and Gerjuoy (1955), Norcross and Spiker (1957), Muehl (1960), Muehl (1961), Gibson *et al.* (1962), Hendrickson and Muehl (1962), Muehl (1962), Staats, Staats and Schutz (1962), King (1964), Georgiades *et al.* (1965), King and Muehl (1965), Marchbanks and Levin (1965), Samuels and Jeffrey (1966), Samuels (1967), Silvaroli and Wheelock (1967).

These experiments in training visual and auditory discrimination thus seem to indicate that such activities may be helpful in the classroom. But how much do specific commercially produced reading readiness materials help children under normal conditions? This was the question in which Ollila was chiefly interested. Before conducting his own experiments, he reviewed seven previous investigations* of commercially published reading readiness programmes. Most of these were concerned with the relative value of the 'formal' methods of commercial materials in comparison with 'informal' experience activity approaches devised by teachers.

Ollila found that these studies were somewhat inconsistent in their findings, but, nevertheless, there were several 'general trends', of which the following was listed first:

'Children who were trained with a formal programme using workbooks with exercises involving gross kinds of visual discrimination such as interpreting pictures achieved about the same as children taught with an informal experience activity approach.'

This statement is reminiscent of Lovell's (1963) research on the relative effects of formal and informal methods in British primary schools. He studied two groups of schools. One group were 'described as informal in the sense that creative work of all kinds is actively encouraged, and considerable use made of the environment in fostering children's interests and in allowing the pupils to follow their own interests as far as possible. Children in such schools were compared with pupils in schools where the learning situation was more directed, and the curriculum followed traditional lines.' Lovell compared the reading attainments in the informal schools with those of the more formal schools.

His first conclusion was similar to that of Ollila's. Lovell states:

'No significant differences have been found between the mean reading scores of children in informal and formal schools, using two age groups in eleven pairs of schools matched for social class.'

But Lovell adds a very interesting comment:

'Overall there is no evidence whatever of any deterioration of reading standards in informal junior schools. Although there is no evidence that these schools bring superior standards in reading, *they may well benefit their pupils in other ways.*' (italics added).

* Ploghoft (1959), Collins (1960), Blakely and Shadle (1961), Hillerich (1965), Schoepenhoester *et al.* (1966), Silberberg (1966), Brzeinski (1967).

The last sentence is extremely important. The educational aim of the creative discovery approach in informal education is much broader than the narrow one of improving reading attainments. Therefore, their success cannot be measured by standardised reading tests alone. So long as there are 'no significant differences' in the test scores of formal and informal schools, the teachers must be free to choose one or the other according to their professional judgment of the effects of such methods on a more general educational basis.

Nonetheless, commercially produced more formal reading readiness programmes are very popular in America, and it seems important to investigate their value more closely. Oddly, such programmes often differ quite widely in their content. Do such differences produce any corresponding differences in the readiness of children who use such programmes? Ollila's experiment looked into this question by comparing three programmes which 'differed to varying degrees in skills taught, materials used, and principles and methods of instruction.' The three programmes are described by Ollila as follows:

1 Readiness Program 'A' (Building Prereading Skills—Kit B Consonants) taught a specific readiness skill—the phoneme-grapheme relationship—in a more traditional method using a teacher's manual, picture and word cards. Special features of the program included the teaching of 15 initial consonants and their sounds, use of picture and oral context clues, and the introduction of three consonants at a time in every set of lessons.

2 Readiness Program 'B' (The First Talking Alphabet) also taught the same specific readiness skills, the phoneme-grapheme relationship, but used a more modern approach that included recorded instruction. Special features of the program included teaching 21 initial and final consonants and digraphs and their sounds, the use of kinesthetic modality and introduction of one consonant or digraph, and teaching all objectives pertinent to that consonant or digraph in each lesson.

3 Readiness Program 'C' (*Frostig Program for the Development of Visual Perception,* Frostig and Horne, 1964) taught the more generalised skills of visual perception and excluded training in phoneme-grapheme relationships. The program taught five visual perceptual skills through the use of various visual-motor workbook exercises.

Ollila taught three groups of kindergarten children, each group by a different one of the above three programmes. He tested readiness both before and after the teaching programme was given. Three tests were used including the *Marianne Frostig Developmental Test of Visual Perception* (Frostig,

Lefever and Whittlesey, 1964) which is related to 'Programme C', of course. The most notable fact in Ollila's findings is how very little the results differed from one group to another. If Ollila's testing is valid, one must ask, were all three programmes training the same skills incidentally despite apparent differences in the materials? Or, were the three programmes equally teaching nothing at all?

The implications of Ollila's research seem important for practical reasons. As Ollila himself recognises:

'The finding of this study may seriously question the relative effectiveness of teaching certain general and specific readiness skills in commercial reading readiness programs. No one training program was more effective in teaching the skill of visual perception, as shown on the visual perception test. This result was of special interest considering that one program was designed specifically to develop visual perception.'

In this statement, Ollila is referring to the fact that the children who used the *Frostig Program for the Development of Visual Perception* scored no better on the *Frostig Developmental Test of Visual Perception* than children in the other groups who used a reading readiness programme other than the Frostig one. Frostig (1968) is modest in her own claims for her visual perception training program, but she does seem to believe that it is helpful for reading. But other investigations of the Frostig programme have not been more encouraging than Ollila's. Jacobs *et al.* (1968) found that, while the Frostig programme seemed to improve visual perception in general it did not lead to any improvement in reading in the first or second grades. Wingert (1969) concluded from his research that the Frostig programme seemed to help develop 'visual motor abilities' but 'this type of programme does not seem to transfer to other more school-related activities.'

Ollila's study has an even wider and more general implication. Before engaging in a programme to change the child to fit him better for the reading task, we should be sure that the change really will make him more ready for reading. Because visual discrimination ability is highly correlated with reading progress, this does not prove that the former is the cause of the latter. All we know from a correlation is that the two activities are in some way or other connected. Thus a general training in visual perception may have no effect on reading readiness.

An even more glaring example of this correlation fallacy is the conclusion which has been jumped to regarding children's knowledge of the names of letters of the alphabet. As we noted in Chapter 5, a number of investigations have shown that pre-school tests of knowledge of letter-names correlate more highly with first grade reading attainments than any other measure of reading readiness. Other studies which confirm that letter-name knowledge is the best single predictor of first grade achievement in reading include those of Barrett (1965), de Hirsch *et al.* (1966), Bond and Dykstra (1967) and Dykstra (1967).

Barrett was quite clear about the limitation of his own research results. He realised that the ability to recognise letters of the alphabet 'may be a reflection of a rich experience with a variety of written materials which enable children to learn to recognise letters.' The same rich experience helps such children to become better readers, later. Therefore, Barrett warned:

'It should not be inferred from this study that teaching children to recognise letters by name will necessarily ensure success in beginning reading.'

But Barrett's warning did not prevent a number of writers from drawing that conclusion too hastily. For example, Chall (1967) states that 'knowing the names of the letters before learning to read helps a child in the beginning stages of learning to read, whether he learns from an approach emphasising code or meaning' (pp. 149–150). As a result, there are dozens of different pieces of apparatus now on the market in America for teaching kindergarten and pre-school children the ABC. One well known children's T.V. show, *Sesame Street*, gives a great deal of attention to the alphabet and the letter-names.

Unfortunately, when this facile conclusion was put to the test, the waste of time and effort it has caused became all too obvious, in three quite separate scientific experiments. Johnson (1970) and Samuels (1970) have tested the effects of training children to name letters of the alphabet, and both reached the same conclusion.

Johnson reports that instruction in letter-names 'resulted in superior letter-name knowledge' but it 'did not result in vocabulary or comprehension reading achievement different from that of the control group' who had no letter-name training.

Samuels reported as follows:

'The results of the two experiments indicate that letter-name knowledge does not facilitate learning to read words made up of the same letters ... The fact that the two studies failed to find facilitation for the letter-name groups on the transfer tasks strongly suggests that letter-name knowledge does not help the student learn to read.'

Ohnmacht (1969) also failed to find any greater improvement in reading achievement in children trained in letter-name knowledge in comparison to a control group who got no such training in his classroom investigation.

It seems astonishing that this alphabetic method should be resurrected in 1970 after being so well interred by Huey (1908) at the beginning of this century. Then he said:

'The alphabet method, used almost universally in Greece and Rome, and in European countries generally until well into the nineteenth century, and which was nearly universal in America until about 1870, is now chiefly of historical interest.'

In Britain, too, Morris (1959) notes that the alphabetic method 'has virtually disappeared in this country'.

Indeed, there were rather obvious practical reasons for dropping the practice of starting with learning the letter-names. As Reid (1966) notes:

'It should perhaps be stressed that the teaching of the letter-names is not being advocated as part of early teaching of reading. Some do advocate it, for instance, Durrell (1956) and Fries (1962), *but the danger of confusion with the basic sounds is considerable* (Reid, 1958).' (italics added)

On the auditory discrimination side, much less has been done to develop methods of training readiness for reading. In British primary schools a good deal of attention is given to informal language development. It was realised many years ago that a silent school or a silent classroom is one in which the child's cognitive growth as well as his linguistic development is being stunted. There seems little doubt that freedom for linguistic experience and exploration is of great value in reading readiness as well as for other aims in education. Reading is relating written language to spoken language. This can hardly be learnt successfully if there is a deficiency in the latter. There will be too much of the writing which cannot be translated into the speaking for real comprehension to take place.

However, this is linguistic growth—not auditory discrimination. In the latter the child must learn to perceive the phonemes in words he hears, for example, that *ball* and *bought* have three sounds, the first two in each word being the same, but the final being different. Obviously children can handle these phonemic computations in their own speech and in their own listening, but they are not usually able to deal with more abstract problems based on such discrimination. Thus a good deal of the business of using auditory discrimination in learning to read is *a matter of cognitive development*, e.g. developing the concept of the phoneme as a unit of speech sound.

The most interesting research on training this kind of auditory discrimination comes from Russia. Elkonin (1963) notes:

'In teaching reading to children of five and six years old the main fact we come up against is that they do not know the sounds of language, do not hear and are unable to distinguish the separate sounds within a word.'

To change the child in this respect in order to fit him better for the reading task, Elkonin has devised a system for making the task more concrete:

'The child pointed to a picture depicting an object under which there was a schema of the sound constitution of the word naming the object made up of horizontal squares for the number of sounds in the word. The child was asked to fill in this schema with counters designating separate sounds, naming each sound'

Later the child performed the activity without the schema, and later still without the counters. The next stage was for the child to be able to name the sounds within a word spoken to him. Other games were added as the children became better able to juggle with the sounds they heard in words.

All of this was done *without written letters*, i.e. before any formal phonics, as such. Elkonin's research showed clearly that this method is very effective in cultivating auditory discrimination readiness for reading.

Elkonin's method, developed originally for the Russian language, has been modified for developing reading readiness in the English language by Downing (1964). His method consists in a set of cards which can be used in a variety of games to develop the same kind of effect described by Elkonin. Gayford (1970) describes some informal activities based on the same principles.

It is important to note that all these activities develop auditory discrimination within the spoken language alone and without any written letters. When the child is familiar with the sounds of language he is ready to learn how those sounds are written—is the underlying principle of this aspect of cultivating readiness. Gjessing's Norwegian research on reading readiness led him to conclude that when the young beginner first approaches the task of learning to process the written form of language:

'What is actually new in the written language is the application of a *new form* of symbols, the written letters. If written symbols are to be used normally, it appears to be highly important that *symbol manipulation* should have reached a certain level in relation to speech development before the pupil is taught the written language.'

Another quite different method of fitting the child for the reading task has been described by Brzeinski (1964). This approach was via the parents, who were provided with a specially prepared guide book of reading readiness activities linked with sixteen T.V. programmes. Reports claim that children helped in this way were much better prepared to begin reading when they arrived in school for the first time. A study by McManus (1964) confirms this finding.

One interesting unplanned result in Brzeinski's experiment brings home the general truth of the effectiveness of co-operation between school and home in helping children to get ready for reading. Some of the children in Brzeinski's control group whose parents did not get the readiness advice by booklet or T.V. were just as advanced as children in the experimental group whose parents did have the special advice. On investigation, it was found that usually these children in the control group came from homes where parents made a regular practice of reading books to them. Durkin also found that this kind of parental help was a factor of importance in her study of children who came to school already able to read.

Another research experiment which brought out the value of parental help for reading readiness was that reported by Willmon (1969). This was an investigation of one aspect of the 'Head Start' programme in Florida. Willmon related the extent of parent participation in the pre-school Head Start activities to their children's subsequent reading readiness as measured by the *Metropolitan Test* administered during their first week in first grade. Her findings were as follows:

'Statistical techniques revealed that the mean group scores of subjects whose parents participated actively were significantly higher than the subjects whose parents did not participate.'

Therefore Willmon recommends 'that teachers provide many varied opportunities for parents to become involved in the school programme.'

Training children via their parents is taken to its extreme form in Doman's (1965) *Teach Your Baby to Read* proposals. His attack on the conventional conception of reading readiness is also notable in another way. He claims that the readiness period occurs not after age six, but long before that. Educators, in his view, have generally started to teach reading too late instead of too early. His theory is related to developments in ethology, particularly to the concept of critical or *sensitive periods* in the development of organisms. Doman posits that in human beings there is a sensitive period for language learning which occurs nearer to the age of two years than six years. Therefore, he claims that 'the earlier a child reads, the better he reads'.

Stevens and Orem (1968) have mustered some indirect evidence for this view. They conclude:

'There appears to be a critical period in humans between the ages of one and five years for learning language. At present, we usually limit the child's experience during this time to spoken language symbols, but there is strong evidence that the same period of time could and should be used for the mastery of visual language symbols.'

These two writers are careful to point out that this 'does not mean that formal reading instruction, such as the child may encounter abruptly upon his entry into the regular first grade, should be introduced into the home or the nursery school environment. . . . If we want our children to read with fluency and understanding, we must devise an environment in which they can learn to read as naturally as they now learn to talk.'

It is doubtful if Doman's method achieves this aim. Apart from the larger print used and the younger age of the child taught, Doman's method is a straightforward individual look and say method, and much evidence has already been cited of 'babies' learning to 'read' in similar ways. The following comment of Diack's (1965) is very apt:

'It would be as well too, for parents who try to teach their babies to read to be aware that the word recognition stage is a very easy one. The trial of the teacher's patience comes when she is trying to get the child to understand what the letters are there for. Children will appear to be able to read long before they are actually able to do so in the full sense of the word.'

The development and understanding of concepts embodied in words comes through experience and takes time to acquire, so although an earlier start to reading may be made using Doman's system, the true reading process cannot be hurried to this great extent, as the reading of words must go hand in hand with the understanding of them.

The fact that *knowledgeable* parents can fit their children better for the task of reading is well-established by such research as that of Brzeinski, McManus, and Durkin, all quoted earlier. But Doman's book does not provide much real assistance for the parent who wants to give help which really will fit the child more for the reading tasks which lie ahead in the everyday life school situation.

A much more useful guide to parents is the little book by Glyn (1964), *Teach Your Child to Read*. On the very first page its author dispels any wrong notions which a parent may have mistakenly read into the title of her book:

'I must emphasise that the assumption that a child is learning to read only when he is given methodical instruction from a reading primer is a totally misguided one. Unfortunately, however, it is an assumption which is often made by parents of young children.'

Glyn continues:

'One of the purposes of this book is to try to clarify such common misunderstanding and to show you some of the ways in which you can, without forcing his pace, help your child to be busy about reading even before he goes to school; how, too, when he is admitted to school, you can assist and co-operate with his teacher who may well be contributing in a similar way to his development in reading.'

What follows in the pages of Glyn's book provides real insight into the creative methods used in the modern British primary school. It is a remarkably good guide for parents who wish to work in harmony with their child's future teachers.

The methods proposed by Glyn are largely directed at fitting the child for the reading activities he will meet when he goes to school, but since such activities in a good British primary school do recognise the other need—to fit the reading to the child— both ways of approaching readiness are found in this book for parents.

FITTING READING TO THE CHILD

This side of the readiness coin is much less evident than the other one described earlier in this chapter, but the 1960s have seen increasing attention being given to this approach to narrowing the gap between the child's developmental stage and the conditions of the learning task. Yet in this period of notable reform in this respect, some educational writers have been remarkably blind to the possibility that 'reading' need not be a fixed quantity, but can be more or less complex according to the needs of the learner. For example, one American educationist declared recently that the superior ability of i.t.a. pupils as compared with t.o. pupils, as shown by the tests in the British research, did not count because they were reading i.t.a. which, he said, was 'not real reading'. Anyone who has seen a child chuckling over a funny storybook printed in i.t.a., can have no doubt as to what that child is doing. If he is 'not reading', what is he doing? By that American educationalist's definition, Russian and Chinese people, for example, are 'not reading' either since their languages do not employ the traditional alphabet and spelling of English. In summary, reading is not a fixed and immutable task. It differs from one language to another and it can be changed within one language to fit the child's needs and so help to close the readiness gap.

A number of methods of fitting reading to the child have been proposed in recent years. One less obvious example is that of McCracken's (1953) New Castle method (named after the town in Pennsylvania which pioneered this approach). In it, the class is taught as a whole from the beginning of the first grade. All new material to be read is first taught by projecting film-strip pictures of the pages of the reading books on to a large screen. After intensive study of the film-strips, the pupils read the corresponding pages in the related reader. McCracken's published results indicate a high degree of success in first grade reading and Lichtenstein (1960) has confirmed its success.

At first sight, this whole class method may seem to ignore readiness altogether, and McCracken (1952) apparently believes that he is doing so, for he writes, 'Are we on the wrong track when we place so much emphasis on readiness for reading? I certainly think so.' But, actually, McCracken's method does change the task to fit it more to the needs of the child in at least one important respect. Many children, when they start school, are more far-sighted at that age and the large screen image of the print allows them to read at a far-point. Thus, albeit incidentally perhaps, McCracken has changed reading to suit the child.

But of much greater significance for our topic in this chapter are the several ways in which 'reading' has been changed in respect of the basic raw material which the young beginner has to learn to process, i.e. the symbols printed on his page or written on the teacher's charts. Although this approach is not new, the past decade has seen much interest in simplifying the alphabet and spelling of English to make it more suitable for young children. During this period, three different approaches to reducing the complexity of the traditional orthography (t.o.) of English have been adopted more and more widely to ease the initial problems of developing reading and writing skills:

1 *Supplementary codes* which retain the t.o. alphabet and spelling but use, for instance, colours to provide a clear and reliable code for English phonemes. The best known examples

are Gattegno's (1962) *Words in Colour* and Jones' (1967) 'Phonetic Colour' systems.

2 *Simplified and regularised alphabets*, in which t.o. is abandoned altogether (except for some letters) and replaced by an entirely fresh alphabet with regular spelling, e.g. Malone's *UNIFON* alphabet (see Ratz 1966).

3 *Transitional alphabets* in which the same regularisation and simplification is attempted, but, as far as possible, without losing similarity to t.o. which is kept as the ultimate goal in learning to read. The outstanding example is the initial teaching alphabet (i.t.a.) devised by Sir James Pitman (1961), with its special design to facilitate transfer from i.t.a. to t.o. once fluency has been established.

All three of these approaches to readiness by fitting the reading task to the child have in common the feature of providing clear and consistent visual experiences of the phonemic structure of English. Any of these systems should make it easier for a child *to understand* the coding function of written or printed symbols. Thus they are in tune with needs revealed by research on an extremely important aspect of readiness. *Cognitive clarity* is much more likely to be achieved successfully through these clear and simple systems for representing English sounds.

Diack (1967) has argued that the same results can be achieved in t.o. by a phonic method in which only consistently spelt words are used, leaving the irregular words till later. But this vocabularly restriction method has the disadvantage of making the language to be read artificial and remote from the child's normal experiences of spoken English, thus widening the gap between the reading task and the child's linguistic experience. In contrast, i.t.a. narrows the gap between the difficulty of the written code and the intellectual ability of the young child and at the same time allows the use of any word in the English language – since they are all spelt consistently in i.t.a. Thus i.t.a. narrows the gap between the reading task and the child in both respects at once, i.e. intellectually and linguistically.

Gattegno's *Words in Colour* and Jones's 'Phonetic Colour' should, in theory allow the same double advantage, but it is not reflected in Gattegno's teaching materials or highly phonic methods. Jones's teaching materials and methods do seem to reflect much closer attention to the child's natural interests and language. But both methods suffer from the possible defect that orientation to a *colour* code is misleading because all normal reading codes which the children must later use are, in fact, black symbols on a white background. If they do meet coloured letters in the normal environment, the colour does not usually have a significance for reading except as some special non-verbal signal, e.g. red for danger. In contrast, i.t.a. orientates children to the task of perceiving differences *in shape*, which is the essential visual basis of reading – not colour.

Most of the evidence on the effectiveness of fitting the reading code to the child comes from the several investigations which have been made of i.t.a. Do these show that i.t.a. is easier and hence more suitable for young beginners than t.o.?

Downing (1967a) conducted two large-scale experiments with i.t.a. which went on for several years in Britain. Both showed conclusively that i.t.a. is very much easier for beginners. For example, at the end of one year, on several tests of reading, i.t.a. pupils could read more than twice as much of the English language in i.t.a. as t.o. pupils could read in t.o.

Recently, the Schools Council in Britain, invited Warburton and Southgate (1969) to review all published investigations of i.t.a. and to conduct a survey of the opinions of teachers in England. Again, the evidence was conclusive. The i.t.a. system was found to be easier for young beginners. The following are the relevant conclusions from the Schools' Council report:

'Among infant teachers who had used i.t.a. there was almost total agreement concerning its favourable effect on children's reading progress. The comments most frequently made by teachers were that i.t.a. enables children to make a good beginning with reading; the task is simpler and consequently children can begin earlier, learn more quickly and achieve greater pleasure and satisfaction in so doing.'

The review of the seventeen published experimental researches on i.t.a. led the authors of the Schools' Council report to note that most people have made the assumption in the past that, if t.o. is what we all use in reading once we have learned the basic processes, then t.o. must be the best system to begin with. But the evidence shows that we have been mistaken in that assumption:

'There is no evidence whatsoever for the belief that the best way to learn to read in traditional orthography is to learn to read in traditional orthography. It would appear rather that the best way to learn to read in traditional orthography is to learn to read in the initial teaching alphabet.'

The Schools' Council report makes it quite clear that i.t.a. is referred to as 'best' because of its simplicity and the way in which it makes the initial learning task *easier for the child*. The conclusion could hardly be otherwise, since in the seventeen experiments reviewed in the Schools' Council report 'all the significant differences were in favour of i.t.a.' in the tests comparing initial learning in i.t.a. with initial learning in t.o.

Even more directly to the point are the two studies of the effects of i.t.a. on *reading readiness* itself. Downing (1963) reported that, in his original experiment, he found an important difference in this respect between his i.t.a. and t.o. groups. In the t.o. group, children aged five years made significantly better progress in learning to read than children of age four. But, in the i.t.a. group, the four-year-olds learned just as well as the five-year-olds. He concluded:

'The majority of four-year-olds may not be able to learn to read traditional orthography, but this does not appear to be true of their ability to learn to read i.t.a.'

Recently, Thackray (1971) has confirmed this conclusion in his large-scale experiment designed specifically to test i.t.a.'s influence in reading readiness. His results confirm that i.t.a. does, to an important degree, narrow the gap between the child's ability and the intellectual problems of learning to read by making the latter easier.

Other research evidence confirms the importance of this *orthography factor* in reading readiness. A recent article by the Japanese neuro-psychiatrist, Kiyoshi Makita (1968), concludes that reading disability is rare in Japan because each letter in Kana script (which children learn on first coming to school) 'is always read in one consistent way', whereas reading disability has an unusually high incidence in the English-speaking countries because 'in English a letter is pronounced in various ways'. Other authors have noted that the traditional orthography of English is more difficult than the conventional way of printing or writing Hebrew (Feitelson 1965), Arabic and Armenian (Hildreth 1965 and 1966, and Diringer 1949), Georgian (Allen 1932 and 1935), German (Preston 1952), Greek (Hildreth 1968), Finnish (Kyostio 1967). Downing (1967b and 1969) has reviewed these and other studies in two other articles. These led to the proposal for an international co-operative study of the problem of the relationships between different languages and the relative difficulty of learning to read and write in them. The results were published in *Comparative Reading* (Downing 1973).

It seems probable that the reading readiness gap between the difficulty of the orthography and the child's abilities at, say, age five differs from one language to another. The role of i.t.a. may be to narrow that gap in English and thus make it more similar to what it is in, for example, Finnish *in this respect*. (The two languages differ in other ways which may affect the width of the readiness gap as well.)

This concept of fitting the reading to the child was always a fundamental basis in the theoretical arguments which Pitman advanced in i.t.a.'s favour, when he first urged its use in Britain. It is odd that this vital point has been overlooked seemingly by some of the American reading specialists who have adopted i.t.a. For example, in apparent conflict with the independent results both of Downing and of Thackray are those of Tanyzer, Alpert and Sandert (1966) which, they say, show that 'introducing a consistent medium such as i.t.a. to kindergarten children in a formal reading programme does not result in significantly better reading and spelling achievement than attained by children who begin formal reading instruction in first grade in i.ta. when both groups are measured (in t.o.) at the end of first grade.'

But another American research found just the opposite result. Shapiro and Willford (1969) obtained significantly superior results from the children who began i.t.a. a year earlier in kindergarten instead of first grade.

The difference in the results is caused by the classical error in the former study of treating 'reading' as a fixed unchangeable entity. In this case it was the 'i.t.a. reading' that was assumed to be constant. Tanyzer and his colleagues used the American i.t.a. *Early-to-Read* series *designed for six-year-olds*. These were given also to the five-year-old kindergarten children in their experiment. In the study of Shapiro and Willford the five-year-olds had i.t.a. materials *designed for five-year-olds*. (The *Downing Readers* and other special i.t.a. materials suited to this age group.) Failure to adjust i.t.a. materials to the age level of the child has been an error in classroom practice also. The same American *Early-to-Read* i.t.a. series for six-year-old beginners was given to Canadian five-year-olds at Halifax, Nova Scotia. The results were so disappointing that i.t.a. was abandoned altogether in that city.

Educators have to be constantly on their guard if they aim to approach readiness by fitting reading to the child. In the experiment of Tanyzer *et al.* and in the introduction of i.t.a. into Halifax, Nova Scotia, the basic error made was to assume that the simplification of the orthography in i.t.a. was all that needed to be done. 'What worked with six-year-olds should work with five-year-olds; it's all i.t.a. reading' seems to have been the assumption. These failures with i.t.a. serve to remind us that readiness is relative to all the many facets of the tasks involved in reading. Narrowing the gap between the difficulty of the reading task and the intellectual development of the child on one dimension does not mean that we can ignore all the other dimensions of readiness.

87

The same reminder applies to this chapter as a whole. The way in which i.t.a. fits the orthography to the child is only one of many ways in which the general principle of this side of the readiness coin can be applied.

For another example, consider the problems we discovered in Chapter 5. If children are unready for reading because they do not understand its *purpose*, then, the 'reading' we introduce them to must be fitted to this need in the child. Clearly, the child should meet real-life examples of the communication and expressive purposes of written language. In all schools, reading can be integrated naturally with other activities which children understand more immediately. For example, five-year-olds enjoy making things to eat. If they share the experience of looking up the recipe with their teacher or with older children who already can read, they learn through such realistic experiences the true purpose of written language. A valuable guide to this aspect of reading readiness is Gayford's (1970) recent book. It provides many helpful practical suggestions for the teacher who strives to make reading relevant for her pupils' own interests and experiences.

This may seem a rather different kind of consideration to that in i.t.a. In a way it is, for i.t.a. is an example of the attempt to adjust the *orthography* to the intellectual capacity of the young beginner. The recipe book suggestion represents an effort to adjust *teaching method* to the child's special needs at this beginning stage. Many other examples will occur to teachers reading this chapter if they accept the importance of the general principle that we should fit the reading to the child.

Chapter 7 An Appraisal of Reading Readiness

The discussion in the preceding chapters of the main factors involved in reading readiness and the ways in which they may be taken into account by teachers and parents indicates the complexity of the concept and the practical difficulty of determining any one point in time at which a child is ready for reading. The magic 'teachable moment' for beginning reading seems impossible to find.

There can be no decisive answer to the question 'When is a child ready for reading?' because there is no single criterion that applies to all children or to all learning situations. Children grow towards readiness for reading at different rates and vary widely in the various abilities, skills and understanding which make for reading readiness; again, reading methods and materials differ from classroom to classroom affecting the threshold requirements of readiness. A more reasonable question would be 'When is *this* particular child ready for *this* particular reading programme?'

However, when classes are large in number, any help the teacher can be given in her task of appraising reading readiness is valuable; in such appraisal it is necessary to consider the many and varied items which contribute to readiness. The three main methods by which teachers in many American schools gather information concerning readiness are:

The use of a reading readiness test.
The use of an intelligence test.
The directed observation of each pupil's behaviour.

Investigations by Robinson and Hall (1942), Kottmeyer (1947), and Henig (1949), among others, have been made to find out which of the above methods is the most predictive if only one is used, and secondly whether a combination of two or all three of the methods is more valid. The research findings are not clear cut, but indicate that when methods are combined the correlation figure is altered by a minimal amount. As to which method is the most predictive, the findings of Robinson and Hall, who analysed the data of over twenty investigations, are still valid as shown by the more recent investigations by Spaulding (1956) and by Bremer (1959) in America, and by Thackray (1965) in Britain. Robinson and Hall found that the median correlation between reading success and these three types of predictive measures were: reading readiness tests ·58, intelligence ·51, and teachers' rating scales ·62. It is notable that the teachers' judgments scored highest in this comparison. However, let us examine each type of measure in turn.

1 *Reading readiness tests*
Since 1930 in America reading readiness tests have become more numerous and are now quite widely used there. These tests are usually group tests consisting of a number of sub-tests of the pencil and paper kind; they are similar to intelligence tests but they differ in that they are directed specifically at skills which the research literature shows are connected with reading. Standish (1959) has analysed eight American reading readiness tests and finds that, of the eight, all use a test of visual discrimination, six use tests of vocabulary, three use motor tests, two use tests of the reproduction of patterns and shapes from memory, and two make use of tests of relationship. Other tests used include: ability to recall a story, ability to remember ideas in sequence, pronunciation, rhyming of words, auditory discrimination, and handedness and eyedness. Examples of some of these devised by Thackray are shown on pages 100–2.

The most widely used reading readiness tests in America are the *Gates Reading Readiness Tests* (Gates 1939), the *Harrison-Stroud Reading Readiness Profiles* (Harrison and Stroud 1956), *the Metropolitan Readiness Tests* (Hildreth and Griffiths 1948) and the *Monroe Reading Aptitude Test* (Monroe 1935a). In addition to general reading readiness tests there are a number of tests used in America which are connected with a basic reading series; these tests are composed of sub-tests and some items relate to the material to be found in the basic readers.

Gates, Bond and Russell (1939), Betts (1948) and Harrison and Stroud (1956), have emphasised the diagnostic value of reading readiness tests. Betts feels that these tests have been a potent factor in furthering interest in reading readiness problems. He argues that, firstly, they make it possible for the teacher to identify specific strengths and weaknesses in certain areas, such as visual and auditory discrimination, background of information, vocabulary, perception of relationships, and secondly, that the fairly specific nature of the tests makes it possible to suggest relevant procedures for developing reading readiness sub-skills.

Another obvious and practical way of finding out if a child is ready to learn something is to try him out on a sample of the learning task and see if he can do it. We might call this the 'try him and see if he can' method. Durrell (1956) although admitting that reading readiness tests predict readiness fairly well suggests a very simple alternative method; he recommends teaching the child some words and then seeing if he can remember them. He suggests that children should be taught from three to ten words, printed on individual cards which bear no identifying marks that may be associated with individual words; after an hour each child is tested individually to see how many words he can remember. Durrell called this measure the 'learning rate' and feels that a child who can remember the words is ready for reading. It is interesting to note that teachers in Britain generally use a similar measure as a guide, though not in any structured way; they introduce the words of the introductory reader to the children and one criteria of readiness for reading is if they can remember the words.

The *Thackray Reading Readiness Profiles* (Thackray and Thackray 1974) are the first original British reading readiness tests to be published. They are group tests designed for use with reception class children soon after they enter school, and provide the teacher with a quick, convenient and reliable measure of vocabulary development, auditory discrimination, visual discrimination and general abilty. But in order to complete these four tests satisfactorily, a child must pay attention and follow directions, and examine the pictures and words in a left to right sequence, so these abilities are also measured in the Profiles. The standardisation was carried out with a population of 5,500 children from urban and rural areas, differing home backgrounds, and from England, Wales, Scotland and Northern Ireland. The raw scores obtained for each test are converted to a grade on a 5-point scale (A, B, C, D and E), relating each child's score to that of the population of 5-year-old children just starting school. The results indicate those children who are strong in all the reading readiness measures and who could learn to read with success at once, and also those children who are weak in all the measures and who must not be hurried into learning to read. However, for the majority of children the Profiles aim to be diagnostic and to provide the teacher with valuable information about her children's reading readiness abilities.

2 *Intelligence tests*
Since general intelligence is an important factor in readiness for reading, and since many have indicated that a certain minimum mental age is necessary for success in reading, group or individual intelligence tests are often used in American schools for appraising readiness for reading. Schonell (1961) feels that for the appraisal of reading readiness with British children, too, mental age is useful. He recommends as possible

individual tests the *Stanford-Binet Intelligence Scale* (Terman and Merrill 1961) and the *Wechsler Intelligence Scale for Children* (1955), and as a group test the *Moray House Picture Intelligence Test* (Mellone 1944). These recommendations are not realistic, however, as British teachers are not permitted to use either the *Stanford-Binet* test or the *Wechsler Intelligence Scale for Children*, and the *Moray House Picture Intelligence Test* is too difficult for children below the age of six.

3 *Directed observation of pupils' behaviour*
Teachers' judgements regarding a child's readiness for reading have been shown to be very sound; as already noted, Robinson and Hall (1942) found a higher median correlation between teachers' ratings and reading success than between the latter and either reading readiness tests or intelligence tests.

The reasons for this are likely to be complex. But obviously a teacher who gets to know her pupils personally soon becomes sensitive to each individual's development in a wide range of aspects of growth—a much wider range than is sampled by either reading readiness tests or tests of general intelligence. Furthermore, our review of the research on intellectual factors in readiness brought out an important area of children's development which is hardly touched on directly by these tests. We are referring to children's cognitive development, and in particular their growth of cognitive clarity regarding the functions and processes of reading. Reading readiness tests are generally deficient in this respect, and intelligence tests are not sufficiently specific to bring out this aspect of readiness. New tests should be developed for this purpose.

Meanwhile the teacher's judgement can include such considerations, although, again, the published guides and inventories are also rather vague as regards this important aspect of child development for reading readiness.

Gray (1956) points out that teachers can observe their children's behaviour in the following ways:
1 Observing the characteristics and behaviour of children in their play activities;
2 Studying during class periods their responses in various learning activities;
3 Getting reports from parents and previous teachers, if any, concerning their interests, language ability, and the general status of their mental, physical, social and emotional development.

Most American writers of books on reading instruction and writers of basal reading schemes, have suggested the form a teacher's record sheet for each child might take, and the ways in which notes on all the important abilities and skills involved in reading readiness, could be recorded. Some useful forms have been suggested by Lamoreaux and Lee (1943), Betts (1946), Russell (1949), Harris (1961) and Gray (1956).

Some of these observation lists are very detailed, others more simple. For example Betts' list is very detailed and covers several pages; the list is divided into major divisions as follows:

1 Social adjustment, which includes checks on attitudes, emotional stability, interests and work habits;

2 Mental maturity, which includes checks on general alertness and ability to relate language and experience;

3 Background of experience, which includes checks on literature, information, school experience and home background;

4 Language adjustment, which includes checks on speech, language usage and reading and writing;

5 Physical qualifications, which includes checks on visual sensation and perception, auditory sensation and perception, nutrition, glandular balance, dentition and health habits;

6 Motor development, which includes checks on rhythm, balance and co-ordination.

A list of a simpler nature is that of Harris, which covers the following:

NAME

AGE

Mental Ability
General Mental Maturity (M.A)
Brightness (I.Q.)
Visual Perception
Auditory Perception

Health
Vision
Hearing
General Health
Physical Maturity
Lateral Dominance

Experience
Cultural Level of Home
Richness of Experience

Language
Vocabulary
Use of Language
Clearness of Speech

Social and Emotional
Family Relationships
Emotional Stability

Self-Help
Group Participation

Interest in Books

Over-all Rating

Schonell (1961) has produced a check list in the form of a printed card for use in British schools which he calls a *Reading Readiness Chart*. It is divided into eleven sections under headings as follows:

1 Mental level
a. Remarks based on class observations
b. Supplementary data—I.Q., mental age
2 Reading Readiness Abilities
a. Remarks based on class observations
b. Reading readiness test results (or results from the use of a reading readiness book)
3 Estimate of experiential background
4 Extent and quality of play with other children
5 a. Ability to listen to what is read
b. Ability to attend to instructions
6 Extent of vocabulary and talk with others
7 Attitude towards books and printed words
8 Social and emotional attitudes
9 Physical Equipment
a. Vision
b. Hearing
c. Speech (accuracy)
d. Physical state (energy)
10 Recommendations as a result of Sections 1 to 9
11 Further progress

Conspicuous in these three examples is the absence of any mention of children's concepts and reasoning abilities of specific importance in the learning-to-read process.

To the best of the authors' knowledge, Schonell's card is not used very widely in Britain, but most infant teachers do make notes of their day-to-day observations of the children in their classes and these records prove very helpful. A more structured form of observation and recording however could prove a valuable aid in judging readiness, particularly if it took more account of the cognitive factors which have been recognised as more important since the work of Piaget. For British teachers, however, such a list still would have to be short and simple. Bearing in mind the relative importance of the factors involved in reading readiness already discussed it should be concerned primarily with general mental ability, the specific abilities of visual discrimination, auditory discrimination, specific cognitive development as regards concepts and reasoning skills required in learning to read, and the cultural aspects of home background.

Many groups of teachers are at present working together to develop different aspects of the curriculum for all types of school. Reading readiness is a very important area of concern to infant teachers, and study groups of infant teachers should be encouraged to draw up simple reading readiness charts embodying the common experience and knowledge of its members; such charts would be readily accepted and of real value.

To provide a starting-point for teachers who wish to develop their own reading readiness chart we propose tentatively the following inventory of factors to be considered in judging a child's preparedness for the tasks involved in the beginning stage of learning to read.

Reading Readiness Inventory

Name

Date of Birth

Date of School Entry

Boy or Girl

Age at School Entry   Years   Months

1 PHYSIOLOGICAL FACTORS

a. *Vision*

    i Has vision been tested?

    ii Is vision normal?

    iii If not, what has been prescribed?

    iv Are there any signs of visual discomfort?

b. *Hearing*

    i Has hearing been tested?

    ii Is hearing normal?

    iii If not, what has been prescribed?

    iv Are there any signs of hearing problems?

c. *Speech*

    i Is speech normal?

    ii If not, what defect is there?

    iii If any defect, what has been prescribed?

d. *Physical State*

    i Is there any physical defect?

    ii Is there normal physical energy?

    iii Is there normal coordination of body movements?

2 ENVIRONMENTAL FACTORS

a. *Home Experiences*

    i Has the child contact with books at home?

    ii Does someone read to him at home?

   iii Do the parents try to help him to read?

   iv If so, *how* do they attempt to do this?

  b. *Cultural Affiliation*

     i Do the parents speak English at home?

    ii If not, what language do they speak?

   iii Does the child speak another language, or in a dialect other than standard English?

   iv If so, which?

3   EMOTIONAL, MOTIVATIONAL AND PERSONALITY FACTORS

a. Has the child any *severe* emotional or personality problems?

b. If so, what are they?

c. Has he a marked dislike for books?

d. What are his *special interests* which may be used to motivate him to use books?

e. Does he know that pleasurable things can be found in books?

4   INTELLECTUAL FACTORS

a. *Cognitive Development*

     i How quick is the child at learning new things?

    ii Does he *understand* why we have a written language?

   iii Does he *understand* the difference between a written word and a picture?

   iv Does he *know the meaning* of 'word', 'letter', 'number', and other technical terms of written language?

    v Does he *understand* that spoken language can be divided up into words and sounds?

   vi Does he *understand* that words can be built up from sounds?

b. *Auditory Discrimination*

     i Can the child hear that two or more words begin with the same sound?

    ii Can he hear that two or more words rhyme?

   iii Can he hear that two or more words end with the same sound?

   iv Can he hear that two or more words have the same sound in the middle?

c. *Visual Discrimination*

     i Can the child match identical sentences in print?

    ii Can he match printed words?

   iii Can he match printed letters?

   iv Can he find small differences in printed words, e.g. dog, bog, or kit, kite?

d. *Language Development*

     i In his own language, or dialect, how fluent is the child?

    ii How extensive is his talk with others having the same language, or dialect?

    iii How extensive is his vocabulary in his own language or dialect?

    iv How fluent is he in standard English?

    v How extensive is his vocabulary in standard English?

In effect, the above represents a summary of what we have found in reviewing the factors related to reading readiness. But it presents more the fitting the child for reading side of the readiness coin. In our final conclusions now we shall emphasise the other aspect—fitting the reading to the child, although, clearly, in using the above readiness inventory, the teacher will not be seeking the impossible 'magic moment' to begin. She will use it more to determine what kind of readiness or reading activities each child needs to make further progress.

CONCLUSIONS AND SUMMING UP

We have just proposed (1975) a *Reading Readiness Inventory* (available as a separate form from the publishers of this book) which teachers can use to organise their knowledge of each child's development in the learning-to-read process. As we pointed out, this inventory is also a summary of our findings from our review of research on this topic. It lists the factors we have found to be important in fitting the child for reading.

We have also concluded in Chapter 6 that readiness does not need to wait for mere biological maturation. There are many ways in which teachers and parents can help their children develop the understandings and sub-skills which are the basis of learning to read. Research has found quite clearly that readiness can be trained to a useful extent.

But we need to reiterate some of the warnings derived from our review of the research. In particular, teachers should beware of naïve conclusions drawn from correlational studies. The outstanding example in the literature of reading readiness is the letter-names fallacy. Although a child's knowledge of letter-names is a good guide to his general level of progress towards readiness, teaching children the letter-names has no effect in improving their abilities in learning to read. A more appropriate type of training would be to provide those rich experiences of natural language which are the probable cause of a child being both good at naming letters at the pre-school stage and good at learning to read when he comes to school. Such language experiences must be *natural*, not the artificial questioning procedures recommended by many teachers' manuals for American reading programmes. Language growth depends on experiences which are really relevant to the child—language which is integrated with his own interests and activities in his natural environment.

Teachers and parents also should view commercial claims for readiness materials or readiness tests with a degree of caution. With regard to published tests, none have proved superior to the professional judgement of the teacher. Indeed, teachers' assessments have been found to be slightly better. Readiness programmes which have been published have also been found in research to be no more than *as good as* informal procedures invented by individual teachers for their own classrooms. We must add that formal readiness programmes are equal to teacher-devised informal activities only as regards formal tests of reading readiness. The informal activities may have other valuable effects, besides.

Our final word must be to emphasise the direction in which educational thought seems to be moving as regards the reading readiness concept. In recent years it has been increasingly recognised that the teacher is the one whose readiness needs evaluating, perhaps even more than the child's. A *teacher's* readiness test would check such questions as:

1 How am I fitting my demands in reading to the child's level of readiness?

2 Do the reading books fit the child's experiences of life in his particular environment?

3 Do the books fit his language or dialect?

4 Do the teaching methods fit the child's level of ability?

5 Does the alphabet in which the child's books are printed fit his needs in cognitive development?

Although they have not applied their theories directly to the teaching of reading, two of the world's leading psychologists have given the lead in developing this more dynamic view of readiness for education in general, Vygotsky (1963) in Russia, and Bruner (1960) in America.

Vygotsky's important contribution is his concept of 'the zone of potential development'. He points out that the usual objective tests of general intelligence or some more specific ability only gives us a *static* picture of the child's actual development at one moment in time. This is useful, but it does not tell us the child's potential in making the next step in developing this ability. Two children may both score the same on such a test. Yet, if we give each of them the same amount of help, one might leap ahead while the other remained at the same level. The difference lies in the 'zone of potential development'. Vygotsky proposes that we can measure this by giving the test twice, once without help, and then with a given amount of assistance. Then we can gauge the child's potential for new learning.

This is rather like Durrell's method which we labelled the 'try him and see if he can' approach, and which many practical teachers have used intuitively. The important lesson we as reading teachers learn from this is that readiness is a dynamic condition *depending upon flexible features of the child and flexible features of the teacher and her methods and materials.*

Bruner begins by attacking the conventional view of readiness as some 'magic moment' before which it is useless to even try to teach the child:

'Experience over the past decade points to the fact that our schools may be wasting precious years by postponing the teaching of many subjects on the ground that they are too difficult.'

Bruner asserts, then:

'The foundations of any subject may be taught to anybody at any age in some form. . . . The basic ideas that lie at the heart of all science and mathematics and the basic themes that give form to life and literature are as simple as they are powerful. To be in command of these basic ideas, to use them effectively, requires a continual deepening of one's understanding of them that comes from learning to use them in progressively more complex forms. It is only when such basic ideas are put in formalised terms as equations or elaborated verbal concepts that they are out of reach of the young child, if he has not first understood them intuitively and had a chance to try them out on his own. The early teaching of science, mathematics, social studies, and literature should be designed to teach these subjects with scrupulous intellectual honesty, but with an emphasis upon the intuitive grasp of ideas, and upon the use of these basic ideas.'

We believe that Bruner's words apply with the greatest possible force to the early stages of learning to read. The teacher who keeps in mind this quotation from Bruner will be constantly aware that reading readiness is a state of the teacher as well as of the child. She will take care, not only to fit the child for reading, but also to fit the reading to the child.

1 VISUAL DISCRIMINATION

a. *of objects*

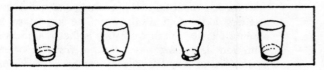

b. *of symbols*

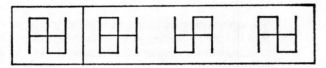

c. *of real or 'nonsense' words*

2 AUDITORY DISCRIMINATION

a. *of consonantal sounds* (*beginnings*)

b. *of vowel sounds* (*endings*)

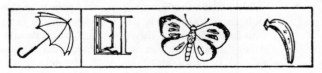

c. *of digraph sounds* (*endings*)

3 VOCABULARY

a. of simple words

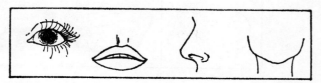

b. of harder specific words

4 MOTOR OCULAR CONTROL (PROGRESSIVE)

 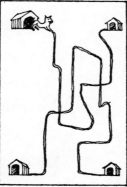 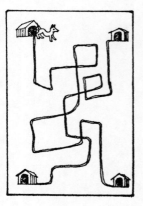

5 SPEECH: ARTICULATION (PROGRESSIVE)

1. poppy	5. brown blocks	9. she sells shells
2. see-saw	6. yellow leather	10. chatter clap chop
3. round about	7. quiet clock	11. physiological
4. lollipop	8. mum mob mop	12. corollary

6 MAKING SENTENCES

Bibliography

ABERNETHY, E. M. (1936) 'Relationship between mental and physical growth.' *Monographs of the Society for Research in Child Development.* **1**, 7, Washington, D.C.: Society for Research in Child Development, National Research Council.

ABIRI, J. O. O. (1969) *World initial teaching alphabet versus traditional orthography.* Ph.D. Thesis, University of Ibadan, Nigeria.

ALLEN, R. V. (1961) 'More ways than one.' *Childhood Education.* **38**, 108–11.

ALLEN, W. E. D. (1932) *The History of the Georgian people.* London: Kegan Paul, Trench, Trubner.

ALLEN, W. E. D. (1935) *The present state of Caucasian studies.* Chipperfield, England: The Georgian Historical Society.

ANDERSON, I. H., and DEARBORN, W. F. (1951) *The Psychology of Teaching Reading.* New York: Ronald Press.

ANDERSON, I. H., and HUGHES, B. O. (1955) 'The relationship between learning to read and growth as a whole.' *School of Education Bulletin.* University of Michigan.

ANDERSON, I. H., HUGHES, B. O., and DIXON, W. R. (1957) 'The rate of reading development and its relation to age of learning to read, sex, and intelligence.' *Journal of Educational Research.* **50**, 481–94.

ANDERSON, M., and KELLY, M. (1931) 'An inquiry into traits associated with reading disability.' *Smith College Studies in Social Work.* **2**, 46–63.

ARTLEY, A. S. (1961) *What is Reading?* (pamphlet). Chicago: Scott, Foresman.

ASHER, E. J. (1935) 'The inadequacy of current intelligence tests for testing Kentucky mountain children.' *Journal of Genetic Psychology.* **46**, 480–86.

BALLARD, P. B. (1922) *Group Tests of Intelligence.* London: Hodder and Stoughton.

BARRETT, T. (1965) 'Predicting reading achievement through readiness tests.' In FIGUREL, J. A. (Ed.) *Reading and inquiry.* Newark, Delaware: International Reading Association.

BELMONT, L., and BIRCH, H. G. (1963) 'Lateral dominance and right-left awareness in normal children.' *Child Development.* **34**, 257–70.

BENDA, C. E. (1954) 'Psychopathology of childhood.' In CAR-

103

MICHAEL, L. (Ed.) *Handbook of Child Psychology*. London: Chapman and Hall.

BENNETT, C. (1938) 'An inquiry into the genesis of poor reading.' *Contributions to Education*. No. 755. New York: Teachers' College, Columbia University.

BETTS, E. A. (1946) *Foundations of Reading Instruction*. New York: American Book.

BETTS, E. A. (1948) 'Remedial and corrective reading: content area approach.' *Education*. **68**, 579–96.

BIGELOW, E. B. (1934) 'School progress of under age children.' *Elementary School Journal*. **35**, 186–92.

BIRD, G. (1927) 'Personality factors in learning.' *Personnel Journal*. **6**, 56–9.

BLAKELY, P. W., and SHADLE, E. L. (1961) 'A study of two readiness for reading programs in kindergarten.' *Elementary English*. **38**, 502–5.

BLANCHARD, P. (1928) 'Reading disabilities in relation to maladjustment.' *Mental Hygiene*. **12**, 772–88.

BLOMMERS, P., KNIEF, L., and STROUD, J. B. (1955) 'The organismic age concept.' *Journal of Educational Phychology*. **46**, 142–50.

BLOOM, B., DAVIS, A., and HESS, R. (1965) *Compensatory Education for Cultural Deprivation*. New York: Holt, Rinehart and Winston.

BLOOMFIELD, L., and BARNHART, C. L. (1961) *Let's Read: a Linguistic Approach*. Detroit: Wayne State University.

BOND, G. L. (1935) 'Auditory and speech characteristics of poor readers.' *Contributions to Education*. No. 657. New York: Teachers' College, Columbia University.

BOND, G. L., and DYKSTRA, R. (1967) *Final Report of the Coordinating Center for First-grade Instruction*. (USOE Project X-001). Minneapolis: University of Minnesota.

BOND, G. L., and TINKER, M. A. (1957) *Reading Difficulties: Their Diagnosis and Correction*. New York: Appleton-Century-Crofts.

BRADLEY, B. E. (1955) 'An experimental study of the readiness approach to reading.' *Elementary School Journal*. **56**, 262–7.

BREMER, N. (1959) 'Do readiness tests predict success in reading?' *Elementary School Journal*. **59**, 222–4.

BRUMBRAUGH, F. (1940) 'Reading Expectancy.' *Elementary English*. **17**, 153–5.

BRUNER, J. S. (1960) *The Process of Education*. New York: Vintage Books.

BRZEINSKI, J. E. (1964) 'Beginning reading in Denver.' *The Reading Teacher*. **18**, 16–21.

BRZEINSKI, J. E. (1967) *Summary report of the effectiveness of teaching reading in kindergarten.* Cooperative research project no. 5-0371. Denver, Colorado: Denver Public Schools.

BURT, C. L. (1922) *Mental and Scholastic Tests.* London: King.

BURT, C. L. (1937) *The Backward Child.* London: University of London Press.

BURT, C. L. (1966) 'Counterblast to dyslexia: disability in reading.' *Association of Educational Psychologists News Letter.* **5**, 2–6.

BURTON, W. H. (1956) *Reading in Child Development.* New York: Bobbs-Merrill.

BUSWELL, G. T. (1937) 'How adults read.' *Supplementary Educational Monographs.* No. 45. Chicago: University of Chicago Press.

CANTOR, G. N. (1955) 'Effects of three types of pretraining on discrimination learning in preschool children.' *Journal of Experimental Psychology.* **49**, 339–42.

CARROLL, M. W. (1948) 'Sex differences in reading readiness at first grade level.' *Elementary English.* **25**, 370–75.

CENTRAL ADVISORY COUNCIL FOR EDUCATION (1967) *Children and their primary schools.* (The Plowden report). London: Her Majesty's Stationery Office.

CHALL, J. S. (1967) *Learning to Read: the Great Debate.* New York: McGraw-Hill.

CLARK, M. M. (1967) 'Laterality characteristics and reading.' *Reading.* 1(3), 3–9.

COLE, L. (1938) *The improvement of reading with special reference to remedial instruction.* New York: Farrar and Rinehart.

COLLINS, M. E. (1960) *Determining the relative efficiency of a particular reading readiness workbook and a teacher-developed program in promoting reading readiness.* M.A. Thesis, De Pauw University.

CORBIN, R. (1965) 'Literacy, literature and the disadvantaged.' *Language programs for the disadvantaged.* Champaign, Illinois: National Council of Teachers of English.

DALTON, M. M. (1943) 'A visual survey of 5 000 schoolchildren.' *Journal of Educational Research.* **37**, 81–94.

DANIELS, J. C., and DIACK, H. (1956) *Progress in Reading.* Nottingham: University of Nottingham Institute of Education.

DAVIDSON, H. P. (1931) 'An experimental study of bright, average and dull children at the four year mental level.' *Genetic Psychology Monograph.* **9**, 119–289.

DAVIDSON, H. P. (1934) 'A study of reversals in young children.' *Journal of Genetic Psychology.* **45**, 452–65.

DAVIS, L. F. et al. (1949) Perceptual Training of Young Children. Evanston, Illinois: Row-Peterson.

DE HIRSCH, K. et al. (1966) Predicting Reading Failure: a Preliminary Study. New York: Harper and Row.

DEAN, C. D. (1939) 'Predicting first grade reading achievement.' Elementary School Journal. 33, 609–16.

DEARBORN, W. F. (1933) 'Structural factors which condition special disability in reading.' Proceedings of the American Association for Mental Deficiency. 38, 266–83.

DEARBORN, W. F., and ROTHNEY, J. W. M. (1941) Predicting the Child's Development. Cambridge, Mass.: Science/Art Publications.

DEARDEN, R. F. (1967) 'Curricular implications of developments in the teaching of reading.' In DOWNING, J., and BROWN, A. L. (Eds.) The Second International Reading Symposium. London: Cassell.

DECHANT, E. V. (1970) Improving the Teaching of Reading. Englewood Cliffs, N.J.: Prentice-Hall.

DELACATO, C. H. (1963) The Diagnosis and Treatment of Speech and Reading Problems. Springfield, Illinois: Thomas.

DEPUTY, E. C. (1930) 'Predicting first grade reading achievement.' Contributions to Education, No. 426. New York: Teachers' College, Columbia University.

DEUTSCH, M. (1960) 'Minority group and class status as related to social and personality factors in scholastic achievement.' Monographs of the Society for Applied Anthropology, No. 2.

DEWEY, J. (1898) 'The primary education fetich.' Forum. 25, 314–28.

DEWEY, J. (1909) How We Think. London: Cambridge University Press.

DEWEY, J. (1916) Democracy and Education. New York: Macmillan.

DEWEY, J. (1926) Science and the Modern World. London: Cambridge University Press.

DIACK, H. (1960) Reading and the Psychology of Perception. Nottingham: Skinner.

DIACK, H. (1965) In Spite of the Alphabet. London: Chatto and Windus.

DIACK, H. (1967) 'Evaluations—3.' In DOWNING, J. et al. The i.t.a. Symposium. Slough, Bucks: National Foundation for Educational Research in England and Wales.

DIRINGER, D. (1949) The Alphabet: a Key to the History of Mankind. London: Hutchinson.

DOLBEAR, K. E. (1912) 'Precocious children.' Pedag. Seminary. 19, 461–91.

DOLCH, E. W. (1950) *Teaching Primary Reading.* Champaign, Illinois: Garrard Press.

DOLCH, E. W., and BLOOMSTER, M. (1937), 'Phonic readiness.' *Elementary School Journal.* 38, 201–5.

DOMAN, G. J. (1965) *Teach Your Baby to Read.* London: Cape.

DOWNING, J. (1963) 'Is a "mental age of six" essential for "reading" readiness?' *Educational Research.* 6, 16–28.

DOWNING, J. (1964) *Auditory Discrimination Cards for the Downing Readers.* London: Initial Teaching Publishing Co.

DOWNING, J. (1966) 'Reading readiness re-examined.' In DOWNING, J. A. (Ed.) *The First International Reading Symposium.* London: Cassell, and New York: John Day, pp. 3–23.

DOWNING, J. (1967a) *Evaluating the initial teaching alphabet.* London: Cassell.

DOWNING, J. (1967b) 'The influence of English orthography on the teaching of reading in English-speaking countries.' In JENKINSON, M. D. *Reading Instruction: an International Forum.* Newark, Delaware: International Reading Association.

DOWNING, J. (1968a) 'Should today's children start reading earlier?' In DOWNING, J., and BROWN, A. L. (Eds.) *The Third International Reading Symposium.* London: Cassell, pp. 16–25.

DOWNING, J. (1968b) 'Today's major problem group—socially disadvantaged children.' In DOWNING, J. A., and BROWN, A. L. (Eds.) *The Third International Reading Symposium.* London: Cassell, pp. 42–66.

DOWNING, J. (1969) 'Comparative reading: a method of research and study in reading.' In FIGUREL, J. A. (Ed.) *Reading and Realism.* Newark, Delaware: International Reading Association.

DOWNING, J. (1970a) 'The development of linguistic concepts in children's thinking.' *Research in the Teaching of English.* 4, 5–19.

DOWNING, J. (1970b) 'Children's concepts of language in learning to read.' *Educational Research.* 12, 106–12.

DOWNING, J. (1972) 'Children's developing concepts of spoken and written language.' *Journal of Reading Behaviour.* 4, 1–19.

DOWNING, J. (1973) *Comparative Reading.* New York: Macmillan, and London: Collier-Macmillan.

DOWNING, J., and THOMSON, D. (1975) 'Sex role stereotypes in learning to read.' *Research in the Teaching of English.* (In the press.)

DURKIN, D. (1959) 'A study of children who learned to read prior to first grade.' *California Journal of Educational Research.* 10, 109–13.

DURKIN, D. (1961) 'Children who learned to read at home.' *Elementary School Journal.* 62, 14–18.

DURKIN, D. (1963) 'Children who read before Grade 1: a second study.' *Elementary School Journal.* 64, 143–8.

DURKIN, D. (1964) 'Early readers—reflexions after six years of research.' *Reading Teacher.* **18**, 3–7.

DURRELL, D. D. (1940) *Improvement of basic reading abilities.* Yonkers: World Book.

DURRELL, D. D. (1956) *Improving Reading Instruction.* New York: World Book.

DURRELL, D. D., and MURPHY, H. A. (1953) 'The auditory discrimination factor in reading readiness and reading disability.' *Education.* **73**, 556–60.

DURRELL, D. D., MURPHY, H. A., and JUNKINS, K. M. (1941) 'Increasing the rate of learning in first grade reading.' *Education.* **62**, 37–9.

DWYER, C. A. (1973) 'Sex differences in reading.' *Review of Educational Research.* **43**, 455–6.

DYKSTRA, R. (1967) *Final report of the continuation of the coordinating center for first-grade reading instruction programs.* (USOE Project 6–1651). Minneapolis: University of Minnesota.

DYKSTRA, R., and TINNEY, R. (1969) 'Sex differences in reading readiness—first-grade achievement and second-grade achievement', pp. 622–8. In FIGUREL, J. A. (Ed.) *Reading and Realism.* Newark, Delaware: International Reading Association.

EAMES, T. H. (1938) 'The ocular conditions of 350 poor readers.' *Journal of Educational Research.* **32**, 10–16.

EDSON, W. H., BOND, G. L., and COOK, W. W. (1953) 'Relationship between visual characteristics and specific silent reading abilities.' *Journal of Educational Research.* **46**, 451–7.

EDWARDS, A. S., and JONES, L. (1938) 'An experiment and field study of North Georgian mountaineers.' *Journal of Social Psychology.* **9**, 317–33.

ELKONIN, D. B. (1963) 'The psychology of mastering the elements of reading.' In SIMON, J. and B. (Ed.) *Educational psychology in the U.S.S.R.* London: Routledge and Kegan Paul.

FAUSTMAN, M. N. (1968) 'Some effects of perception training in kindergarten on first grade success in reading.' In SMITH, H. K. (Ed.) *Perception and reading.* Newark, Delaware: International Reading Association.

FEITELSON, D. (1965) 'Structuring the teaching of reading according to major features of the language and its script.' *Elementary English.* **42**, 870–77.

FENDRICK, P. (1935) 'Visual characteristics of poor readers.' *Contributions to Education.* No. 656. New York: Teachers' College, Columbia University.

FLEMING, C. M. (1943) 'Socio-economic level and test performance.' *British Journal of Educational Psychology.* **12**, 74–82.

FLEMING, C. M. (1900) *Kelvin Measurement of ability in infant classes.* Glasgow: Gibson.

FLESCH, R. (1955) *Why Johnny Can't Read and What You Can Do About It.* New York: Harper Brothers.

FOWLER, W. (1962) 'Teaching a two-year-old to read: an experiment in early childhood learning.' *Genetic Psychology Monographs.* **66**, 181–3.

FRANK, H. (1935) 'A comparative study of children who are backward in reading and beginners in the Infant School.' *British Journal of Educational Psychology.* **5**, 41–58.

FRIES, C. C. (1962) *Linguistics and Reading.* New York: Holt, Rinehart and Winston.

FROEBEL, F. (1887) *The Education of Man.* (Trans. Hailmann, W.N.). New York: Appleton-Century-Crofts.

FROSTIG, M. (1968) 'Visual modality and reading.' In SMITH, H. K. (Ed.) *Perception and Reading.* Newark, Delaware: International Reading Association.

FROSTIG, M., and HORNE, D. (1964) *The Frostig Program for the Development of Visual Perception.* Chicago: Follett.

FROSTIG, M., LEFEVER, W., and WHITTLESEY, J. R. B. (1964) *The Marianne Frostig Development Test of Visual Perception.* 3rd ed. Palo Alto, California: Consulting Psychologists Press.

FURNESS, E. L. (1956). 'Perspective on reversal tendencies.' *Elementary English.* **33**, 38–41.

GAINES, F. P. (1941) 'Interrelation of speech and reading disabilities.' *Elementary School Journal.* **40**, 605–13.

GARDNER, D. E. M. (1948) *Testing Results in the Infant School.* London: Methuen.

GATES, A. I. (1924) 'The nature and educational significance of physical status, and of mental, physiological, social and emotional maturity.' *Journal of Educational Psychology.* **15**, 329–58.

GATES, A. I. (1936) 'Failure in reading and social maladjustment.' *Journal of the National Education Association.* **25**, 205–6.

GATES, A. I. (1937) 'The necessary mental age for beginning reading.' *Elementary School Journal.* **37**, 497–508.

GATES, A. I. (1939) *Gates Reading Readiness Tests.* New York: Teachers' College, Columbia University.

GATES, A. I. (1941) 'The role of personality maladjustment in reading disability.' *Journal of Genetic Psychology.* **59**, 77–83.

GATES, A. I. (1949) *The Improvement of Reading.* 3rd Ed. New York: MacMillan.

GATES, A. I. (1961) 'Sex differences in reading ability.' *Journal of Educational Research.* **36**, 594–603.

GATES, A. I., and BOND, G. L. (1936) 'Reading readiness: a study of factors determining success and failure in beginnng reading.' *Teachers' College Record.* **37**, 678–85.

GATES, A. I., BOND, G. L., and RUSSELL, D. H. (1939) *Methods of Determining Reading Readiness.* New York: Teachers' College, Columbia University.

GATTEGNO, C. (1962) *Words in Colour.* Reading, Berks: Educational Explorers Limited.

GAVEL, S. R. (1958) 'June reading achievement of first grade children.' *Journal of Education, Boston University.* **140**, 30–43.

GAYFORD, O. (1970) *i.t.a. in primary education.* London: Initial Teaching Publishing Co.

GEORGIADES, N. P. *et al.* (1965) 'To read or not to read—in kindergarten.' *Elementary School Journal.* **65**, 306–11.

GESELL, A., and AMATRUDA, C. S. (1941) *Developmental Diagnosis in Normal and Abnormal Child Development.* New York: Paul. B. Hoeber.

GESELL, A., and LORD, E. E. (1927) 'A psychological comparison of nursery-school children from homes of low and high income status.' *Pedagogical Seminary.* **35**, 339–56.

GIBSON, E. J. *et al.* (1962) 'A developmental study of the discrimination of letter-like forms.' *Journal of Comparative and Physiological Psychology.* **55**, 897–906.

GJESSING, H. (1967) 'The concept of reading readiness in Norway.' In JENKINSON, M. D. (Ed.) *Reading Instruction: An International Forum.* Newark, Delaware: International Reading Association.

GLASS, G. V., and ROBINS, M. P. (1967) 'A critique of experiments on the role of neurological organization in reading performance.' *Reading Research Quarterly.* **3**, 5–51.

GLYN, D. M. (1964) *Teach Your Child to Read.* London: Pearson.

GOODMAN, K. S. (1969) 'Dialect barriers to reading comprehension.' In BARATZ, J. C., and SHUY, R. W. (Eds.) *Teaching Black Children to Read.* Washington, D.C.: Center for Applied Linguistics, pp. 14–28.

GOODMAN, K. S. (1970) 'Psycholinguistic universals in the reading process.' *Journal of Typographic Research.* **4**, 103–10.

GORDON, H. (1924) 'Mental and scholastic tests among retarded children.' *Board of Education Pamphlet,* No. 44. London: Her Majesty's Stationery Office.

GRAY, W. S. (1956) *Teaching of Reading and Writing: an International Survey.* Paris: UNESCO, and London: Evans Bros.

HALLGREN, B. (1950) 'Specific dyslexia (congenital word blindness).' *Acta Psychiatrica et Neurologica*, Supplement No. 65, Copenhagen.

HARRINGTON, Sister M. J., and DURRELL, D. D. (1955) 'Mental maturity versus perception abilities in primary reading.' *Journal of Educational Psychology*. 46, 375–80.

HARRIS, A. J. (1957) 'Lateral dominance, directional confusion and reading disability.' *Journal of Psychology*. 44, 283–94.

HARRIS, A. J. (1961) *How to Increase Reading Ability*. 4th edition. New York: Longmans, Green.

HARRISON, M. L. (1939) *Reading Readiness*. Boston, Mass.: Houghton Mifflin.

HARRISON, M. L., and STROUD, J. B. (1956) *Harrison-Stroud Reading Readiness Profiles*. Boston, Mass.: Houghton Mifflin.

HAYES, E. (1933) 'Why pupils fail.' *Educational Method*. 13, 25–8.

HENDRICKSON, L. N., and MUEHL, S. (1962) 'The effect of attention and motor response pretraining on learning to discriminate b and d in kindergarten.' *Journal of Educational Psychology*. 53, 236–41.

HENIG, M. S. (1949) 'Predictive value of a reading readiness test and of teachers' forecasts.' *Elementary School Journal*. 50, 41–6.

HILDRETH, G. (1933) 'Information tests of first-grade children.' *Childhood Education*. 9, 416–20.

HILDRETH, G. (1934) 'Reversals in reading and writing.' *Journal of Educational Psychology*. 25, 1–20.

HILDRETH, G. (1950) *Readiness for School Beginners*. Yonkers, N.Y.: World Book.

HILDRETH, G. (1958) *Teaching Reading*. New York: Holt, Rinehart and Winston.

HILDRETH, G. (1965) 'Lessons in Arabic.' *Reading Teacher*. 19, 202–10.

HILDRETH, G. (1966) 'Armenian children enjoy reading.' *Reading Teacher*. 19, 433–45.

HILDRETH, G. (1968) 'On first looking into a Greek Primer.' *Reading Teacher*. 21, 453–63.

HILDRETH, G. M., and GRIFFITHS, N. L. (1948) *Metropolitan Readiness Tests*. Yonkers, N.Y.: World Book.

HILLERICH, R. L. (1965) 'Studies in reading readiness.' In FIGUREL, J. A. (Ed.) *Reading and Inquiry*. Newark, Delaware: International Reading Association.

HILLIARD, G. E., and TROXELL, E. (1937) 'Informational background as a factor in reading readiness and reading progress.' *Elementary School Journal*. 38, 255–63.

HINSHELWOOD, J. (1917) *Congenital Word-blindness*. London: H. K. Lewis.

HOLMES, J. A. (1962) 'When should and could Johnny learn to read?' In FIGUREL, J. A. (Ed.) *Challenge and Experiment in Reading*. New York: Scholastic Magazines.

HOLMES, J. A. (1968) 'Visual hazards in the early teaching of reading.' In SMITH, H. K. (Ed.) *Perception and Reading*. Newark, Delaware: International Reading Association, pp. 53–61.

HUEY, E. (1908) *The Psychology and Pedagogy of Reading*. New York: Macmillan.

HYMES, J. L. Jr. (1958) *Before the Child Reads*. New York: Row, Peterson.

INGLIS, W. B. (1949) 'The early stages of reading: a review of recent investigations.' In THE SCOTTISH COUNCIL FOR RESEARCH IN EDUCATION. *Studies in Reading*, Vol. 1. London: University of London Press.

JACOBS, J. *et al.* (1968) 'A follow-up evaluation of the Frostig Visual-Perceptual Training Program.' *Educational Leadership*. **26**, 169–75.

JENSEN, M. B. (1943) 'Reading deficiency as related to cerebral injury and to neurotic behaviour.' *Journal of Applied Psychology*. **27**, 535–45.

JOHNSON, D. D. (1973) 'Sex differences in reading across cultures.' *Reading Research Quarterly*. **9**, 67–86.

JOHNSON, R. J. (1970) *The effect of training in letter names on success in beginning reading for children of differing abilities*. Paper presented at the 1970 convention of the American Educational Research Association.

JONES, J. K. (1967) *Research Report on* Colour Story Reading. London: Nelson.

KELLEY, M. L. (1965) 'Reading in the kindergarten.' In FIGUREL, J. A. (Ed.) *Reading and Inquiry*. Newark, Delaware: International Reading Association.

KENNEDY, H. (1942) 'A study of children's hearing as it relates to reading.' *Journal of Experimental Education*. **10**, 238–51.

KENNEDY, H. (1954) 'Reversals, reversals, reversals.' *Journal of Experimental Education*. **23**, 161–70.

KING, E. M. (1964) 'Effects of different kinds of visual discrimination training on learning to read words.' *Journal of Educational Psychology*. **55**, 325–33.

KING, E. M., and MUEHL, S. (1965) 'Different sensory cues as aids in beginning reading.' *The Reading Teacher*. **19**, 163–8.

KIRK, S. A. (1965) 'Language, intelligence, and the educability of the disadvantaged.' *Language Programs for the Disadvantaged*. Champaign, Illinois: National Council of Teachers of English.

KONSKI, V. (1955) 'An investigation into differences between boys and girls in selected reading readiness areas and in reading achievement.' *The Reading Teacher.* **8**, 235–7.

KOSINSKI, W. (1957) 'Die Myopie als variköses Syndron Der Augen.' *Klinische Monatsblätter für Augenheilkunde.* **130**, 266–70.

KOTTMEYER, W. (1947) 'Readiness for reading.' *Elementary English,* **24**, 355–60.

KYOSTIO, O. K. (1967) 'Reading research at the kindergarten level in Finland.' In DOWNING, J., and BROWN, A. L. *The Second International Reading Symposium.* London: Cassell.

LADD, M. R. (1933) 'The relation of social, economic and personal characteristics to reading ability.' *Contributions to Education* No. 582. New York: Teachers' College, Columbia University.

LAMOREAUX, L. A., and LEE, D. M. (1943) *Learning to Read Through Experience.* New York: Appleton-Century Crofts.

LATHAM, W. (1968) 'Are today's teachers adequately trained for the teaching of reading?' In DOWNING, J., and BROWN, A. L. (Eds.) *The Third International Reading Symposium.* London: Cassell.

LEE, E. S. (1951) 'Negro intelligence and selective migration: a Philadelphia test of the Klineberg hypothesis.' *American Sociological Review.* **16**, 227–32.

LENNON, R. (1950) 'The relation between intelligence and achievement test results for a group of communities.' *Journal of Educational Psychology.* **41**, 301–8.

LEVERETT, H. M. (1957) 'Vision test performance of school children.' *American Journal of Ophthalmology.* **44**, 508–19.

LICHTENSTEIN, J. (1960) 'The New Castle reading experiment in Cleveland.' *Elementary English.* **37**, 27–8.

LINEHAM, E. B. (1958) 'Early instruction in letter names and sounds as related to success in beginning reading.' *Journal of Education, Boston University.* **140**, 44–8.

LOBAN, W. (1965) 'A sustained program of language learning.' *Language Programs for the Disadvantaged.* Champaign, Illinois: National Council of Teachers of English.

LOVELL, K. (1963) 'Informal v. formal education and reading attainments in the junior school.' *Educational Research.* **6**, 71–6.

LYNN, R. (1963) 'Reading readiness and the perceptual abilities of young children.' *Educational Research.* **6**, 10–15.

MCCARTHY, D. A. (1935) 'Some possible explanations of sex differences in language development and disorders.' *Journal of Psychology.* **35**, 155–60.

MCCLAREN, V. (1950) 'Socio-economic status and reading

ability: a study in infant reading.' *Studies in Reading*, Vol. 2. Edinburgh: Scottish Council for Research in Education, pp. 1–62.

MCCLELLAND, W. (1942) *Attainment and necessity: Selection for secondary education*. (Publication No. 19 of the Scottish Council for Research in Education.) London: University of London Press. pp. 232–6.

MCCRACKEN, G. (1952) 'Have we over-emphasized the readiness factor?' *Elementary English*. **29**, 271–6.

MCCRACKEN, G. (1953) 'The New Castle reading experiment: a terminal report.' *Elementary English*. **130**, 13–21.

MCLAUGHLIN, K. L. (1928) *First Grade Readiness and Retardation*. Los Angeles, California: The Research Committee of the California Kindergarten—Primary Association.

MCMANUS, A. (1964) 'The Denver pre-readng project conducted by WENH-TV.' *Reading Teacher*. **18**, 22–6.

MACMEEKEN, A. M. (1939) 'Ocular dominance in relation to developmental aphasia.' *Publications of the W. H. Ross Foundation for the study of the Prevention of Blindness*. London: University of London Press.

MCNEIL, J. D., and KEISLER, E. R. (1963) 'Value of the oral response in beginning reading: an experimental study using programmed instruction.' *British Journal of Educational Psychology*. **33**, 162–8.

MCNEIL, J. D., and STONE, J. (1965) 'Note on teaching children to hear separate sounds in spoken words.' *Journal of Educational Psychology*. **56**, 13–15.

MAKITA, K. (1968) 'The rarity of reading disability in Japanese children.' *American Journal of Orthopsychiatry*. **38**, 599–614.

MALMQUIST, E. (1969) 'Textning och vanlig skrivstil, Experimentella studier.' *Research Reports*, No. 14. Linköping, Sweden: National School for Educational Research.

MALMQUIST, E. (1970) 'A decade of reading research in Europe, 1959–1969: a review.' *Journal of Educational Research*. **63**, 309–29.

MANOLAKES, G., and SHELDON, W. D. (1955) 'The relation between reading-test scores and language-factors intelligence quotients.' *Elementary School Journal*. **55**, 346–50.

MARCHBANKS, G., and LEVIN, H. (1965) 'Cues by which children recognize words.' *Journal of Educational Psychology*. **56**, 57–61.

MELLONE, M. A. (1944) *Moray House Picture Intelligence Test*. London: University of London Press.

MILES, T. R. (1967) 'In defence of the concept of dyslexia.' In DOWNING, J., and BROWN, A. L. *The Second International Reading Symposium*. London: Cassell.

MINISTRY OF EDUCATION (1950) *Reading Ability: Some Sugges-*

tions for Helping the Backward. (Pamphlet No. 18). London: Her Majesty's Stationery Office.

MINISTRY OF EDUCATION (1957) *Standards of Reading 1948 to 1956.* (Pamphlet No. 32). London: Her Majesty's Stationery Office.

MONROE, M. (1935a) *Monroe Reading Aptitude Tests.* Boston, Mass.: Houghton Mifflin.

MONROE, M. (1935a) *Monroe Reading Aptitude Tests.* New York: Houghton-Mifflin.

MONROE, M. (1935b) 'Diagnosis and treatment of reading disabilities.' *34th Yearbook of the National Society for the Study of Education.* Chicago: University of Chicago Press.

MORPHETT, M. V., and WASHBURNE, C. (1931) 'When should children begin to read?' *Elementary School Journal.* **31**, 496–503.

MORRIS, J. M. (1959) *Reading in the Primary School.* London: Newnes.

MORRIS, J. M. (1966) *Standards and Progress in Reading.* Slough, Bucks: National Foundation for Educational Research in England and Wales.

MUEHL, S. (1960) 'The effects of visual discrimination pretraining on learning to read a vocabulary list in kindergarten children.' *Journal of Educational Psychology.* **51**, 217–21.

MUEHL, S. (1961) 'The effects of visual discrimination pretraining with word and letter stimuli on learning to read a word list on kindergarten children.' *Journal of Educational Psychology.* **52**, 215–21.

MUEHL, S. (1962) 'The effects of letter-name knowledge on learning to read a word list on kindergarten children.' *Journal of Educational Psychology.* **53**, 181–6.

NATIONAL COUNCIL OF TEACHERS OF ENGLISH (1965) *Language Programs for the Disadvantaged.* Champaign, Illinois: National Council of Teachers of English.

NATIONAL SOCIETY FOR THE STUDY OF EDUCATION (1925) 'Report of the National Committee on Reading.' *Twenty-fourth Year Book of the National Society for the Study of Education.* Bloomington, Indiana: Public School Publishing Co.

NEFF, W. S. (1928) 'Socio-ecomonic status and intelligence.' *Psychological Bulletin.* **35**, 727–57.

NEWMAN, H. H., FREEMAN, F. N., and HOLZINGER, K. J. (1937) *Twins: a Study of Heredity and Environment.* Chicago: University of Chicago Press.

NICHOLSON, A. (1958) 'Background abilities related to reading success in first grade.' *Journal of Education, Boston University.* **140**, 7–24.

NORCROSS, K. J., and SPIKER, C. C. (1957) 'The effects of type of stimulus pretraining on discrimination performance in pre-school children.' *Child Development.* **28**, 79–84.

OHNMACHT, D. D. (1969) *The effects of letter-knowledge on achievement in reading in the first grade.* Paper presented at American Educational Research Association's convention.

OLLILA, L. (1970) *The effects of three contrasting readiness programs on the readiness skill of kindergarten boys and girls.* Ph.D. Thesis, University of Minnesota.

OLSON, A. V. (1958) 'Growth in word perception abilities as it relates to success in beginning reading.' *Journal of Education, Boston University.* **140**, 25–36.

OLSON, W. (1959) *Child Development.* Boston, Mass.: D. C. Heath.

OLSON, W. C. (1940) 'Reading as a function of the total growth of the child.' In GRAY, W. S. (Ed.) *Reading and pupil development.* (Supplementary Educational Monographs, No. 51.) Chicago: University of Chicago Press.

OLSON, W. C., and HUGHES, B. O. (1942) 'The concept of organismic age.' *Journal of Educational Research.* **35**, 525–7.

OLSON, W. C., and HUGHES, B. O. (1944) 'Concepts of growth—their significance to teachers.' *Childhood Education.* **21**, 53–63.

ORTON, S. J. (1929) 'The sight reading method of teaching reading as a source of reading disability.' *Journal of Educational Psychology,* **20**, 135–43.

PARK G. E., and BURRI, C. (1943) 'The effect of eye abnormalities on reading difficulty.' *Journal of Educational Psychology,* **34**, 420–30.

PATRICK, G. T. (1899) 'Should children under ten learn to read and write?' *Popular Science Monthly.* **54**, 382–92.

PECK, L., and MCGLOTHLIN, L. E. (1940) 'Children's information and success in first-grade reading.' *Journal of Educational Psychology.* **31**, 653–64.

PESTALOZZI, J. H. (1898) *How Gertrude Teaches Her Children.* (Trans. Holland, L. E., and Turner, F. C.) 2nd Ed. Syracuse, N.Y.: Bardeen.

PETERSON, I. (1937) 'The reading readiness program of the Ironwood public schools.' *Elementary School Journal.* **37**, 438–46.

PIAGET, J. (1959) *The Language and Thought of the Child.* Third edition. London: Routledge and Kegan Paul.

PITMAN, I. J. (1961) 'Learning to read: an experiment.' *Journal of the Royal Society of Arts.* **109**, 149–80.

PITMAN, Sir J., and ST JOHN, J. (1969) *Alphabets and Reading.* London: Pitman.

PLOGHOFT, M. H. (1959) 'Do reading readiness workbooks promote readiness?' *Elementary English.* **36**, 424–6.

POTTER, M. (1949) 'Perception of symbol orientation and early reading success.' *Contributions to Education,* No. 939. New York: Teachers' College, Columbia University.

PRESCOTT, C. A. (1955) 'Sex difference in Metropolitan readiness test results.' *Journal of Educational Research.* **48**, 605–10.

PRESTON, R. C. (1952) 'Comparison of word-recognition skill in German and in American children.' *Elementary School Journal.* **53**, 443–6.

RATZ, M. S. (1966) *UNIFON: a design for teaching reading.* Racine, Wisconsin: Western Publishing Educational Services.

RAYBOLD, E. (1929) 'Reading readiness in children entering first grade.' *Third Yearbook of the Psychology and Educational Research Division.* School Publications No. 185. Los Angeles, California: Los Angeles City School District, pp. 98–101.

REID, J. F. (1958) 'A study of thirteen beginners in reading.' *Acta Psychologica.* **14**, 295–313.

REID, J. F. (1966) 'Learning to think about reading.' *Educational Research,* **9**, 56–62.

ROBINSON, F. P., and HALL, W. E. (1942) 'Concerning reading readiness test.' *Bulletin of the Ohio Conference on Reading.* No. 3.

ROBINSON, H. (1946) *Why Pupils Fail in Reading.* Chicago: University of Chicago Press.

ROSENBERGER, P. (1967) 'Visual recognition and other neurologic findings in good and poor readers.' *Neurology.* **17**, 322.

ROUSSEAU, J. J. (1957) *Émile.* (Translator, B. Foxley). London: Dent.

RUSSELL, D. H. (1949) *Children Learn to Read.* Boston: Ginn.

RUSSELL DAVIS, D., and CASHDAN, A. (1963) 'Specific Dyslexia.' *British Journal of Educational Psychology.* **33**, 80–82.

SAMUELS, F. (1943) 'Sex differences in reading achievement.' *Journal of Educational Research.* **36**, 594–603.

SAMUELS, S. J. (1967) 'Attentional process in reading: the effect of pictures on the acquisition of reading responses.' *Journal of Educational Psychology.* **58**, 337–42.

SAMUELS, S. J. (1970) *Letter-name versus letter-sound knowledge as factors influencing learning to read.* Paper presented at the 1970 Convention of the American Educational Research Association.

SAMUELS, S. J., and JEFFREY, W. E. (1966) 'Discriminability of words and letter cues used in learning to read.' *Journal of Educational Psychology.* **57**, 337–40.

SCHAEFFER, M. S., and GERJUOY, I. R. (1955) 'The effect of

stimulus naming on the discrimination learning of kindergarten children.' *Child Development*. **26**, 231–40.

SCHENK-DANZINGER, L. (1967) 'The concept of reading readiness in Austria.' In JENKINSON, M.D. (Ed.) *Reading instruction: an international forum*. Newark, Delaware: International Reading Association.

SCHILDER, P. (1944) 'Congenital alexia and its relation to optic perception.' *Journal of Genetic Psychology*. **65**, 67–8.

SCHOEPENHOESTER, H., BARNHART, R., and LOOMER, W. M. (1966) 'The teaching of prereading skills in kindergarten.' *The Reading Teacher*. **19**, 352–7.

SCHONELL, F. J. (1940) 'The relation of reading disability to handedness and certain ocular factors.' *British Journal of Educational Psychology*. **10**, 227–37 and **11**, 20–27.

SCHONELL, F. J. (1942) *Backwardness in the Basic Subjects*. Edinburgh: Oliver and Boyd.

SCHONELL, F. J. (1961) *The Psychology and Teaching of Reading*. 4th Ed. Edinburgh: Oliver and Boyd.

SCOTT, C. M. (1947) 'An evaluation of training in readiness classes.' *Elementary School Journal*. **48**, 26–32.

SHAPIRO, B. J., and WILLFORD, R. E. (1969) 'i.t.a.—kindergarten or first grade?' *Reading Teacher*. **22**, 307–11.

SHAW, J. H. (1964) 'Vision and seeing skills of pre-school children.' *Reading Teacher*. **18**, 33–6.

SHELDON, W. D., and CARILLO, L. (1952) 'Relation of parents, home and certain developmental characteristics to children's reading ability.' *Elementary School Journal*. **52**, 262–70.

SILBERBERG, M. C. (1966) *The effect of formal reading readiness training in kindergarten on development of readiness skills and growth in reading*. Ph.D. Thesis, University of Minnesota.

SILVAROLI, N. J., and WHEELOCK, W. H. (1966) 'An investigation of auditory discrimination training for beginning readers.' *The Reading Teacher*. **20**, 247–51.

SILVAROLI, N. J., and WHEELOCK, W. H. (1967) 'Visual discrimination training for beginning readers.' *The Reading Teacher*. **21**, 115–20.

SISTER MARY NILA (1940) 'An experimental study of progress in first grade reading.' *Catholic University of America Educational Research Bulletins*. Vol. 12.

SISTER MARY NILA (1953) 'Foundations of a successful reading program.' *Education*. **73**, 543–55.

SISTER MARY OF THE VISITATION (1929) 'Visual perception in reading and spelling.' *Catholic University of America Educational Research Bulletin*. **4**, p. 48.

SMITH, D. E. P., and CARRINGTON, P. M. (1959) *The Nature of Reading Disability*. New York: Harcourt-Brace.

SMITH, N. B. (1950) 'Readiness for reading, II.' *Elementary English.* **27**, 91–106.

SOUTHGATE, V. (1959) *Southgate Group Reading Test 1.* London: University of London Press.

SPAULDING, G. (1956) 'The relationship between performance of independent school pupils on the Harrison-Stroud reading readiness profiles and reading achievement a year later.' *Educational Records Bulletin.* no. 67. 73–6.

SPINLEY, B. M. (1953) *The Deprived and the Privileged.* London: Routledge and Kegan Paul.

STAATS, C. K., STAATS, A. W., and SCHUTZ, R. E. (1962) 'The effects of discrimination pretraining on textual behavior.' *Journal of Educational Psychology.* **53**, 32–7.

STANDISH, E. J. (1959) 'Readiness to read.' *Educational Research.* **12**, 29–38.

STEVENS, G. L., and OREM, R. C. (1968) *The Case for Early Reading.* St Louis: Warren H. Green.

STEWART, W. A. (1969) 'On the use of negro dialect in the teaching of reading.' In BARATZ, J. C., and SHUY, R. W. (Eds.) *Teaching Black Children to Read.* Washington, D.C.: Center for Applied Linguistics, pp. 156–219.

STROUD, J. B. (1956) *Psychology in Education.* New York: Longmans, Green.

SWANSON, D. E., and TIFFEN, J. (1936) 'Betts' physiological approach to the analysis of reading disabilities as applied to the college level.' *Journal of Educational Research.* **29**, 433–48.

TANYZER, H., ALPERT, H., and SANDERT, L. (1966) *Beginning reading—the effectiveness of i.t.a. and t.o.* (Report to the Commissioner of Education). Washington, D.C.: U.S. Office of Education.

TAX, S. (1965) 'Group identity and educating the disadvantaged.' *Language programs for the disadvantaged.* Champaign, Illinois: National Council of Teachers of English.

TEEGARDEN, L. (1932) 'Tests for the tendency to reversals in reading.' *Journal of Educational Research.* **27**, 81–97.

TERMAN, L. M. (1918) 'An experiment in infant education.' *Journal of Applied Psychology.* **2**, 219–28.

TERMAN, L. M. (1919) *The Measurement of Ability.* London: Harrap.

TERMAN, L. M., and MERRILL, M. (1961) *Stanford-Binet Intelligence Scale.* London: Harrap.

TERMAN, L. M., and ODEN, M. (1947) *The Gifted Child Grows Up. Genetic Studies of Genius.* Vol. 4. Stanford, California: Stanford University Press.

THACKRAY, D. V. (1965) 'A study of the relationship between

some specific evidence of reading readiness and reading progress in the infant school.' *British Journal of Educational Psychology.* **35**, 252–4.

THACKRAY, D. V. (1971) *Readiness to Read with i.t.a. and t.o.* London: Geoffrey Chapman.

THACKRAY, D. V. and L. E. (1974) *Reading Readiness Profiles.* London: University of London Press.

THORNDIKE, E. L. (1913) *An Introduction to the Theory of Mental and Social Measurements.* New York: Teachers' College, Columbia University.

TINKER, M. (1932) 'Diagnostic and remedial reading.' *Elementary School Journal.* **33**, 307.

TINKER, M. (1934) 'Remedial methods for non-readers.' *School and Society.* **40**, 524–6.

VERNON, M. D. (1957) *Backwardness in Reading.* London: Cambridge University Press.

VERNON, M. D. (1962) 'Specific dyslexia.' *British Journal of Educational Psychology.* **32**, 143–50.

VERNON, P. E. (1961) *The Structure of Human Abilities.* London: Methuen.

VIITANIEMI, E. (1965) 'Differences in reading between the sexes, I–II.' *Education and School (Kasvatus ja Koulu).* **51**, 122–31 and 173–80.

VORMELAND, O. (1967) *Begynnerundervisningen i norsk og regning cited in* MALMQUIST, E. (1970) 'A decade of reading research in Europe, 1959–1969: a review.' *Journal of Educational Research.* **63**, 309–29.

VYGOTSKY, L. S. (1962) *Thought and Language.* Cambridge, Mass.: M.I.T. Press.

VYGOTSKY, L. S. (1963) 'Learning and mental development at school age.' In SIMON, B. and J. (Ed.) *Educational Psychology in the U.S.S.R.* London: Routledge and Kegan Paul.

WARBURTON, F. W., and SOUTHGATE, V. S. (1969) *i.t.a.: an independent evaluation.* London: Chambers and Murray.

WECHSLER, D. (1955) *Wechsler Intelligence Scale for Children.* New York: Psychological Corporation.

WHIPPLE, G. (1966) 'Inspiring culturally disadvantaged children to read.' In FIGUREL, A. J. (Ed.) *Reading and Inquiry.* Newark, Delaware: International Reading Association.

WILLMON, B. J. (1969) 'Reading readiness as influenced by parent participation in Head Start programs.' In FIGUREL, J. A. (Ed.) *Reading and Realism.* Newark, Delaware: International Reading Association.

WINGERT, R. C. (1969) 'Evaluation of a readiness training program.' *The Reading Teacher*. **22,** 325–9.

WITTENBORN, J. R. (1946) 'Correlates of handedness among college freshmen.' *Journal of Educational Psychology*. **37,** 161–70.

WITTY, P., and KOPEL, D. (1936a) 'Heterophoria and reading disability.' *Journal of Educational Psychology*. **27,** 222–30.

WITTY, P., and KOPEL, D. (1936b). 'Preventing reading disability: the reading readiness factor.' *Educational Administration and Supervision*. **28,** 401–18.

WITTY, P., and KOPEL, D. (1936c) 'Factors associated with the etiology of reading disability.' *Journal of Educational Research*. **29,** 449–59.

WITTY, P., and KOPEL, D. (1939) *Reading and the Educative Process*. Boston: Ginn.

WOODY, C., and PHILLIPS, A. J. (1934) 'The effects of handedness on reversals in reading.' *Journal of Educational Research*. **27,** 651–62.

WOLFRAM, W. A., and FASOLD, R. W. (1969) 'Toward reading materials for speakers of Black English: three linguistically appropriate passages.' In BARATZ, J. C., and SHUY, R. W. (Eds.) *Teaching Black Children to Read*. Washington, D.C.: Center for Applied Linguistics. pp. 138–55.

YATES, A. (1954) 'The teaching of reading from the researcher's point of view.' *Child Education*. **31,** 12.

YOAKAM, G. A. (1955) *Basal Reading Instruction*. New York: McGraw-Hill.

YOUNG, N., and GAIER, E. I. (1951) 'Implications in emotionally caused reading retardation.' *Elementary English*. **28,** 271–5.

Author index

Abernethy, E. M., 17, 103
Abiri, J. O. O., 19, 103
Allen, R. V., 43, 103
Allen, W. E. D., 86, 103
Alpert, H., 87, 119
Amatruda, C. S., 25, 110
Anderson, I. H., 16, 17, 103
Anderson, M., 36, 103
Artley, S., 9, 103
Asher, E. J., 39, 103

Ballard, P. B., 12, 103
Barnhart C. L., 118
Barrett, T., 77, 103
Belmont, L., 28, 103
Benda, C. E., 60, 61, 103
Bennett, C., 33, 36, 104
Betts, E. A., 19, 51, 52, 53, 90, 93, 104
Bigelow, E. B., 53, 104
Birch, H. G., 28, 103
Bird, G., 46, 104
Blakely, P. W., 74, 104
Blanchard, P., 46, 104
Blommers, P., 17, 104
Bloom, B., 39, 104
Bloomfield, L., 9, 104
Bloomster, M., 53, 107
Bond, G. L., 31, 33, 50, 58, 70, 77, 90, 104, 108, 110
Bradley, B. E., 61, 71, 104
Bremer, N., 89, 104
Brumbaugh, F., 47, 104
Bruner, J. S., 14, 98, 99, 104
Brzeinski, J. E., 74, 80, 81, 104
Burri, C., 31, 116
Burt, C. L., 12, 24, 26, 36, 105
Burton, W. H., 32, 47, 105
Buswell, G. T., 26, 105

Cantor, G. N., 73, 105
Carrillo, L., 36, 118
Carrington, P. M., 25, 118
Carroll, M. W., 17, 105

Cashdan, A., 24, 117
Central Advisory Council for Education, 37, 105
Chall, J. S., 77, 105
Clark, M. M., 28, 105
Cole, L., 31, 105
Collins, M. E., 74, 105
Cook, W. W., 31, 108
Corbin, R., 39, 41, 105

Dalton, M. M., 31, 105
Daniels, J. C., 68, 105
Davidson, H. P., 28, 55, 105
Davis, A., 39, 104
Davis, L. F., 73, 106
de Hirsch, K., 77, 106
Dean, C. D., 53, 106
Dearborn, W. F., 17, 27, 29, 103, 106
Dearden, R. F., 9, 106
Dechant, E. V., 46, 106
Delacato, C. H., 29, 106
Deputy, E. C., 51, 106
Deutsch, M., 39, 43, 106
Dewey, J., 12, 106
Diack, H., 13, 54, 61, 68, 81, 84, 106
Diringer, D., 86, 106
Dixon, W. R., 17, 103
Dolbear, K. E., 54, 61, 106
Dolch, E. W., 53, 107
Doman, G. J., 80, 81, 107
Downing, J., 37, 44, 52, 60, 64, 65, 68, 79, 85, 86, 87, 107
Durkin, D., 55, 81, 107, 108
Durrell, D. D., 14, 18, 57, 58, 61, 68, 78, 90, 99, 108, 111
Dwyer, C. A., 21
Dykstra, R., 18, 77, 104, 108

Eames, T. H., 31, 108
Edson, W. H., 31, 108
Edwards, A. S., 39, 108
Elkonin, D. B., 79, 108

Subject index